In Pursuit of Profit

BOOKS AND TAPES BY CHRISTINE HARVEY

Secret's of the World's Top Sales Performers

In Pursuit of Profit... with Bill Sykes

Successful Selling

Successful Motivation in a Week

Public Speaking and Leadership Building

"Can A Girl Run For President?" -You have the Power to Influence Your World Around You

Power Talk – Video or Audio

Can A Girl Run For President? – Video or Audio

3 Steps to Business and Personal Success – Audio

Christine Harvey's books are published in 22 languages worldwide. Check your local bookstore under *author's name*. Titles may differ on translated versions.

In Pursuit of Profit

...The Ultimate Sales and Marketing
Success Guide

by
Christine Harvey

With Bill Sykes

INTRINSIC PUBLISHING
TUCSON, ARIZONA   LONDON, ENGLAND

INTRINSIC PUBLISHING

USA
P.O. Box 26040, Tucson, Arizona 85726 USA
Tel: 1-520-325-8776   Fax: 1-520-325-8743
London
20 Station Road, West Drayton, Middx, England UB7-7BY
Tel. 441-895-431-471   Fax 441-895-422-565

10 9 8 7 6 5 4 3 2 1
Manufactured in the United States of America
ISBN: 1-931031-08-8

Publisher's Cataloging-in-Publication
(Provided by Quality Books, Inc.)

Harvey, Christine.
    In pursuit of profit : --the ultimate sales and
marketing success guide / by Christine Harvey with Bill
Sykes. -- 1st U.S. paperback ed.
    p. cm.
    Includes index.
    ISBN: 1-931031-08-8

    1. Selling. 2. Marketing. 3. Success in business.
I. Sykes, Bill (William) II. Title.

HF5438.25.H37 2001   658.85
                            QBI01-200491

Distributed By:
Seven Hills Book Distributors
1531 Tremont Street, Cincinnati, Ohio 45214
Tel: 800-545-2005 Fax: 888-777-7799
www.sevenhillsbooks.com

About the Authors

Christine Harvey

Christine Harvey is a businesswoman in demand worldwide as a speaker and lecturer. She is author of six books on business and leadership, published in 22 languages plus syndicated articles in the *Los Angeles Times* and 100 other major newspapers and magazines.

She was the first woman and first American to Chair a London Chamber of Commerce and the first American, other than a US President, invited to address the Parliament of Czechoslovakia after Communism fell. She is a trainer to the US military and companies worldwide. She is former Director of a venture capital company and past Chair of an investment partnership.

While living in England she served on a Business Enterprise Board launched by Prince Charles and founded *The Most Promising Businesswoman Award.*

She is a Founding Benefactor of the International Center of the National Speakers Association in the US, former Council member, and founding President of the Paris -Brussels Chapter of the Professional Speakers Association of Europe and sponsored Brussels Capital Toastmasters.

She served as international director of Zonta International, a 36,000 member service organization devoted to enhancing the status of women in over 60 countries, with United Nations consultative status. She was a charter member of Zonta London 2 with former Prime Minister Margaret Thatcher as Honorary Member. She is on the Board of NORAGS, the American Girl Scouts of Europe.

In broadcasting, she hosts *One on One with Christine Harvey - People Making a Difference in Government, Politics and the Community on* Sundays at 2 PM US Mountain Time on 91.3 FM, accessible by internet worldwide on www.KXCI.com. Television programs she's hosted include the half hour special *The Heart and Soul of Leadership* filmed in Bosnia and *Power Talk, a 30 part leadership training* for AFN, American Forces Network in Europe

She serves as Chair of the Advisory Board for International Business Studies at Pima College, plus a state legislature campaign committee, the board of the Sunbelt World Trade Association and is Founder and Chair of a Mayoral support group. She and her husband live in Tucson Arizona and have three children, Laurie, Darrin and Tom.

Bill Sykes

Bill Sykes is the founder and principal of Sykes Consultants that specializes in organizational development consulting for professional service firms, family owned businesses and other companies. Bill Sykes uses his marketing and organizational skills to help companies improve their results. He is described as "a person whose undying enthusiasm makes him a valued colleague," and by his clients as having "a unique ability to bring people together constructively to enhance the results of all concerned."

His consulting work with his own firm, and collaboration with Christine Harvey's firm, Intrinsic Marketing employs his ability to get things done through people. His clients in organization development include professional partnerships and industrial and consumer companies. Along with Christine Harvey, he has founded the highly successful 'Develop Effective Sales' Seminars for personal and company development.

Bill Sykes gained corporate experience in marketing and human resources at Horlicks Pharmaceuticals and with the Beecham group. Later, with Black and Decker, he held the position of Corporate Director of Personnel based in the U.S. with previous responsibility for their Pacific International Operations. His expertise in overseas business took him to the Far East, North and South America, and Europe.

He is active in educational and community affairs and has particular interest in counseling executives. His expertise in personality profiles as they relate to organizational development and to fulfillment on and off the job brings him to addressing community and seminar groups.

Bill is British, and was educated at Sedbergh in England before gaining a Diploma in Management Studies. He is a Fellow of the Institute of Directors, where he is a member of their training faculty. Bill was a contributing author to 'The Communication Advantage' published by the American Institute of Certified Public Accountants. Bill and his family lived in America for 15 years. In 1992 he returned to England with his wife, Angela, and two sons, James and Charles. They now live in Malmesbury, Wiltshire in England.

Dedication

To the clients who have brought these stories alive, and to our readers and audiences who report how they're putting these principles into action. And to you the reader for your diligence in business, which benefits us all.

Contents

PART V

Six Ways To Stop Losing Business Needlessly

PART VI

How To Analyze Your Current Situation And Develop Areas Of Improvement

PART VII

Successes And Failures In Overseas Markets

PART VIII

Consolidating Your Forward Plan

Preface

How—and Why— This Book Was Written

Bill Sykes and I were introduced to each other by one of the advisors at the Institute of Directors in London. Since Bill was British living in America, and I was American living in Britain, we saw similar problems and opportunities that companies face in selling overseas.

The Institute knew what my company, Intrinsic Marketing, was doing in sales training and export assistance, and they thought Bill could assist us with clients who wanted to develop sales outlets or licensing relationships in the U.S., and vice-versa.

From the beginning, Bill and I have looked closely at the problems companies had in their business development. What makes them fail? What helps them succeed? Just as the principles of successful people formed a pattern, so did those of successful businesses.

Certain patterns ran through large and small companies, regardless of their business. Some were manufacturers. Some were service companies. Some were professional groups. We wanted to spread the word about the successes so that the patterns could be adopted by all companies and modified to their needs. It seemed pointless to re-invent the wheel when workable principles already existed.

The result was the development of an intensive seminar to help all directors, managers and sales executives to sell better and increase profits. We addressed not only the people in sales--we addressed everyone who could influence sales. Since 75% of all business is lost on the first contact with a company, we knew that everyone affects sales--service, finance, production--they all play a part. Their ability to motivate people and to get their message across dramatically affects company performance.

In the following pages, you'll see examples of ways people have used these principles in their lives and their businesses. You'll see people who have dramatically increased their business against all odds, people who have gained positions of leadership and community recognition, people whose valuable ideas are influencing others. You'll see the same principles being used successfully in the U.S., England, Japan, Canada, and Australia--around the globe.

The examples have been chosen to give you the insight and inspiration to push the principles into action. They'll help you to increase business by positioning your company, your product, and your ideas in the most effective way.

The course members on our seminars who learn the principles are usually amazed at how quickly they get results. One director of a pharmaceutical company told us that he picks out a new principle regularly to work on. Gradually the principles become incorporated into his management practices. "One of the principles, the one on using benefits," he said, "brought me a 25% increase in sales in the first three months."

The principles described in this book are not theoretical, untested concepts. They are practical, tried and tested practices that work for large companies, small companies, or individuals. They are practices that can be used to obtain immediate results.

The world needs input from us all. You'll find that this book has a strong motivational bent. What does that have to do with management, marketing, sales and *the pursuit of profit*, you might ask?

The answer is this. Having the best solution is not enough. We must also inspire people to take action. Only then will we reach our highest goals. The principles in this book do just that.

When I was in school, I was taught that the road to success was through knowledge. When I was in my teens, I started to question this 'fact.'

I looked at the successful people around me, and it was clear that they were people who could motivate others. They were people who could get their ideas across effectively. Many people with excellent ideas and education were not making their points heard and were therefore not influencing decisions. Good potential leadership was being lost.

This became obvious when I saw others wait until the meeting was over to express their ideas. Often these ideas were better than the ones brought out during the meeting.

From this point on I studied successful. I saw that people used specific principles to influence and decision making.

I started to use the principles in my own career. Despite the fact that there were three unemployed teachers for every employed teacher, I used the principles to get a teaching position, even though I had no previous experience. I used them later to get an executive position in advertising, and then the computer field. Eventually I used the principles to start three of my own businesses.

Later my consulting and training business spread internationally and in 1990 after the Communists left Eastern Europe, we trained 40,000 people in free enterprise management and marketing. I was invited to address the Czechoslovakian Parliament on the privatization of industry. I traveled to Asia and throughout Europe and trained over 100,000 people in sales, marketing, management and public speaking...always using these principles.

I lived in Europe and became Chairman of a London Chamber of Commerce, the first woman and first American elected to that position. I started a scholarship program for young women and a foundation for leadership. I wrote six books which were translated into twenty-two languages. It was a thrill for me to see the principles I had learned from others work in all areas of my own life, then the lives of others as the seminars and books spread across national boundaries, with *In Pursuit of Profit* being published in eight languages.

But the greatest impact the methods made on me when I used them in teaching before I went into business. The school principal called me into his office to tell me that I was being as signed 'a group of low-achieving troublemakers.' You can imagine my reaction as a new teacher. "How will I motivate them?," I asked myself.

I decided to use these same principles which you'll read about in this book.. I decided to 'sell' the students on the idea of achievement.

It worked. Several teachers commented on the students' performance to me. One asked, "What's been happening to those students? I've never seen them care about learning before. Today I even saw some of them studying for your exam during my class!"

At the end of the semester, even I was amazed to find that the six worst school troublemakers were, without exception, all high achievers.

I had *not* focused only on transmitting facts. I focused on helping them motivate themselves. I'd helped them channel their energy into achievement. When they learned that achievement was possible, they started their own upward spiral. It kept going and it fed on itself. It was more self-rewarding than their previous downward spiral. That one year's experience taught me more about motivation and selling than any single experience I have had.

Everyone has wants and needs that must be met. Selling and success in life comes from finding out the needs of others and then helping them fulfill those needs.

Our aim is to get the best ideas and principles into circulation for the good of all. This will help people achieve the maximum potential for themselves, their company, their family, and their community. We wish you all the very best in continued success. Please feel free to write to us with examples of how you've used the principle in this book, so we can share your stories in future books and seminars.

Christine Harvey
Email: ChristineHarvey@Compuserve.com
Website: www.ChristineHarvey.com
Tel US: (520) 325-8733, Fax US: (520) 325-8743
Tel UK: 01895-431 471, Fax UK: 01895-422 565

In collaboration with

Bill Sykes
Email: WASykes@aol.com
Tel UK: 01666-824 211
Fax UK: 01666-825 229

PART 1

FUNDAMENTAL FACTS YOU SHOULD KNOW ABOUT SALES

Chapter 1

Maximize the Contribution Of Ourselves and Others

When I started my consulting and training company, I hired management trainees from various parts of the world. They came for work experience during their college years or just after graduation and stayed for several months. It was critical that I get them up to speed quickly. They typically had no business experience and we needed them contributing to their maximum ability as fast as possible.

During that time, I discovered a method that increased their confidence and skill enormously. I had them record in a small notebook two things they liked doing, or felt a sense of satisfaction at the end of each day.

What do you think happened? Without exception, regardless of their nationality, they were unable at first to acknowledge the good things. They were embarrassed or they got so burdened down with their inabilities that they couldn't at first, think of good points.

SELL SELF DEVELOPMENT

But we persisted. It was my job to sell them on self-development. In fact, that's the first job of every manager. If we can optimize the self-development and contribution of our employees, we have a win-win situation. I said things like, "Look, at the beginning of the week you were terrified of the phone. Now you're doing so well."

ACKNOWLEDGE STRENGTHS AND WEAKNESSES

After a week of recording two things a day, they had ten strengths or things they enjoyed. After a month, they had 40. A trend started to develop.

They saw things about themselves that they never knew. We saw things about them we wouldn't otherwise know. Their self-esteem grew. So did their contribution to our company.

They looked at their strengths and weaknesses honestly and openly. They tried to improve their weaknesses and ride on their strengths.

Soon, they were able to talk on the phone and in person, to presidents of our client companies around the world. They loved the challenges.

SELL HIGH LEVEL RESPONSIBILITY

They soon learned to tackle high level responsibilities. After they left, they wrote to say how extraordinarily their confidence grew and how their goals progressed.

In the course of life, we meet many types of people. Not all are successful. Unfortunately, many haven't learned to be as honest with themselves. They spend more time covering up the weaknesses than improving the strengths. They haven't realized they can't be all things to all people. In trying to do that, they destroy their own confidence.

People are a little like businesses. If we don't identify the strength, we can't make best use of it. This is true for ourselves and employees. But developing strengths requires pushing and stretching beyond comfort zones.

We all know from past experience that we feel best about ourselves when we're reaching new heights and accomplishing new goals.

PUSH THE CHALLENGE THRESHOLD

Emerson summed up the reason quite nicely when he said, "Fear defeats more people than any one single thing in the world."

When we look at people who achieve the greatest success in their fields, we see that they are constantly pushing their challenge threshold to new heights. In the process they gain invaluable practice, experience, and skill that helps them in every area of life.

We need people like this when we pursue profit. But they are not lurking in every doorway waiting to be hired. They have to be developed.

INFLUENCE OTHERS TO DEVELOP PATTERNS OF HIGHEST ACHIEVEMENT

The question is how to keep others and ourselves moving through the challenge thresholds. Why not emulate the most successful?

Isn't life too short to reinvent the wheel each time we set out to do things? Surely we can advance faster if we take the best methods and adapt them to our own needs.

That's exactly why we've written this book. To bring people the best methods of the successful, which can be adapted quickly and effectively--for maximum results.

DON'T WAIT FOR OTHERS

Early in our marriage, my husband Tom and I had a chance to take a trip on the S. S. France ocean liner. I won the trip in an international sewing competition earlier that year. Little did I know how this trip would shape our lives.

We were thrilled and apprehensive at the same time. It would be our first time traveling on a ship, and we wondered what the other people would be like. We were poor struggling students at the time. What would they have in common with us, we wondered?

The S. S. France was magnificent. From the deck to the dining room, the service was superb. The decor was fabulous.

The first night of the voyage we entered the elegant dining room. Each passenger was introduced from the top of the stairs, then we proceeded to our tables. Ours was a table for eight, and we met Dr. and Mrs. Lyle, from Fort Worth, Texas, a couple whose attitude would change our life.

The Lyle's radiated something special: a warmth and a sincerity of conviction that most people didn't have. We discovered that Dr. Lyle was in his 70's and had already contributed much to the medical world in his lifetime. It didn't bother him that the Great Depression had taken away his hard-earned wealth. He just started again.

DON'T LET EXCUSES HOLD YOU BACK

He told us, "You can't be afraid to do things you want to do. You can't make excuses and hold yourself back." The Lyles went on to tell us how they liked doing things for their church and their community. Their contributions were endless.

Dr. Lyle worried a lot about young people. If his patients started smoking when they were young, he would get out a pencil and paper and say, "Look, here's how much money you can save over 40 years if you stop smoking now." The sum was tremendous. He didn't lecture them on health. He gave them an incentive.

He tried to get people to plan ahead in their lives. If they were worried about money, as most people were, he told them to save before they spent. "If you wait to start saving until after you stop spending, you'll find there never is any left," he said. "You have to save first. You have to do it now, no matter how small your income is," he told them.

DON'T LET FEAR HOLD YOU BACK

Dr. Lyle told us about how, some years ago, he made plans to start a hospital. He had invited several doctors to join him in the venture. Many of the doctors were far younger, and had a long future ahead of them. The venture was sound financially, and it would benefit the community tremendously.

Despite the sound prospects, the other doctors hesitated. Fear held them back, but it didn't hold back Dr. Lyle. "If you're going to make major accomplishments in life, you have to take action. You can't wait for those around you."

BELIEVE NOTHING IS IMPOSSIBLE

Some years later, Dr. and Mrs. Lyle's attitude still rang in our ears: "You just have to work hard, do what you know is right, and believe that anything is possible." When Tom and I moved from California to New Jersey, the Lyles suggested that we pass through Colorado and stay at their dude ranch. They wouldn't be there, but their staff would attend to us. Naturally, we jumped at the chance.

The setting of the ranch in the Rocky Mountains was gorgeous. Our children, then ages three, six, and seven, thought they were in heaven. We got to know the staff, and they talked to us about Dr. Lyle.

They said, "You know, that man thinks anything is possible. He wanted to put a lake in here for fishing and everybody told him it was impossible. He didn't listen. He just kept searching until he found someone who thought it was possible."

"Yes," I thought, "these are the people who make communities great, who create jobs and put their wealth to work to benefit all." Yes, making the impossible happen does make sense after all. It happens to those who use courage and conviction.

TAKE STEPS DAILY TO MAXIMIZE CONTRIBUTION

It happened to Walt Disney. He risked his fortune three times in life convincing bankers that animated cartoons and a fun park for adults and kids, called Disneyland, made sense. It happened to Madame Curie when she spent nights awake in her laboratory with the conviction that a new element could be discovered. To make the impossible happen, we have to take the first step. As the old adage says, "A journey of a thousand miles begins with a single step." We don't know what our capabilities are until we try, nor what they'll develop into as we stretch our challenge threshold.

I remember when I was twelve, my mother suggested I take a sewing class. No, in fact, she insisted I take a sewing class. I was terrified. "I won't know anyone or anything. How can I possibly go?" I protested. She won the battle and I went.

Little did I know that a few years later, my new skill would land me that first trip to Paris on the S. S. France in competition with 40,000 people from the Singer Company. That trip led me to Dr. Lyle's philosophies. Without that trip to Paris, I wouldn't have moved to Europe later, and probably not have worked in international business.

The first step is most important. The issue for all of us is to take steps daily to maximize the contribution of ourselves and others.

Today, in my conference speaking and corporate training, I have the opportunity to work with a large number of company directors. They tell us their goals for motivating and training their people for higher performance. The most successful have several things in common.

PERSONAL TRAITS OF THE SUCCESSFUL

1. They are people who have their end goal clearly in mind.
2. They are people who believe that anything is possible.
3. They are people who have enthusiasm and who take action immediately.
4. They are mission oriented.

When I interviewed John Barfield, former Counselor of the American Embassy in Taiwan, on my radio program, he endorsed this fact. He said, "The people who are chosen for highest appointments are mission oriented problem solvers. Our job is to find these rare 'mission oriented' people and influence them".

Successful people are those who don't settle for second best in their own performance--they always stretch themselves to new thresholds.

Undoubtedly, you who are in *pursuit of profit* already possess many of the qualities. It's people like you to whom Bill Sykes and I address our thoughts. For it is you who will make a difference in this world--in crashing through new thresholds--and encouraging others to do the same.

The first lesson of sales is to be able to motivate. Motivate yourself, motivate staff. Motivate the buyer, even your boss.

As you read this book, you'll find an action sheet at the end of each chapter. With this you can plan your unique action steps as you pursue profit--in sales, in marketing, in management, in motivation and in life.

Best of success in your journey!

Remember this fundamental fact about sales:

Success follows those who motivate themselves and others to highest achievement.

ACTION SHEET
Chapter 1

Ideas for Development:

1. Use the small book system to help people record two things they enjoyed or felt a sense of satisfaction from at the end of each day.
2. Help them see a trend in their strengths in order to build skills.
3. Encourage yourself and others to keep pushing the challenge threshold – move out of your comfort zone daily.
4. Don't wait for others – take action on your own goals.
5. Believe nothing is impossible.
6. List other points here:
7.
8.

Of the above ideas, which one is likely to yield the best results?

What percentage of sales (or performance) increase could realistically be expected?

How long would it take: to develop the idea? to get results?

Who would have to be involved?

What date should we start?

What is the first step I should take?

Chapter 2

Give Them the Facts
to Make Their Decision

It doesn't matter whether we're selling ideas, a service or a product. If we're going to win the buyer over, we must have the facts about our product.

What credibility do we have with buyers, if we don't have the facts about our own product? The buyer is likely to say, "If this person hasn't got the facts, I'm wasting my time. I might as well go someplace else." Isn't this true in every industry from domestic appliances to aerospace?

Think back, for example, to the last time you went out to buy an electrical appliance. Were the salespeople knowledgeable or did you have to read the literature yourself and compare the features of one model to another?

Maybe your experience was like mine. I spent one Saturday going from one store to another, looking for a dishwasher. "I want the one that runs the quietest," I told the sales clerk. "I don't know much about these machines," I was told in the first store. "Oh, you won't find that out," I was told in the second, "We only know what's printed on the leaflet." The third store had no one available to talk to. Their sales people were tied up in another department so long that I decided not to wait.

Finally I stumbled into one last department store. There was a lady in the appliance department who really knew her stuff. "This one has three cycles, runs 50 minutes maximum. This one has a special filter," and so she continued about each machine. "What about the quietest?" I asked. "I want a quiet one for my apartment so it won't disturb me in the next room." She didn't hesitate with her answer: "Oh, in that case, you want this machine. It had the quietest rating of all machines in the consumer report that was just published last month." Voila! I was a happy customer. Her product knowledge gave me confidence and I ended my search. She made the sale in five minutes while the other three lost out.

LIVE AND BREATHE PRODUCT
– BECOME AN AUTHORITY

I'm sure I'm not her only satisfied customer. I'm certain that this woman has a high sales performance because she has taken the time and trouble to get to know her product. As I talked to her, I had the feeling she could have continued to give me any fact or figure I needed.

If you think that the lady selling the dishwasher has nothing to do with you, stop and think again. You have to give your buyers the facts to make their decision. You have to prove you can offer the benefits the customer needs, whether you're in banking, stock market trading, accounting, medicine, engineering, consulting or other services--just as those who have a product do.

During one of our seminars for Lloyd's Financial Futures, one attendee said he thought it was easier to talk about the features and benefits of a service than of a product. Decide it's easy to relate the benefits of your product or service to your customer's needs and it will be!

Think back to the dishwasher saleswoman. She had taken the time and trouble to study the features of each product, to read consumer reports--to live and breathe the product--until she was an authority. I would have hired her on the spot. She was one of the few people who understood the real importance of having all the facts about products in order to sell effectively. And why not? Surely our trade is worth studying. To do less is to deny ourselves our own potential!

I had a special need: I wanted a quiet machine. The next customer will be just as awkward: he or she will have special needs. All customers have special needs. The more facts we have, the more customers we can appeal to.

If this aspect of sales is so self-evident, why aren't all salespeople blossoming with facts like this woman? Why haven't they all taken the time and trouble to learn everything they can, until they are authorities?

Perhaps management hasn't made this aspect of sales so self-evident to their people. Perhaps they haven't stopped to realize it themselves. It doesn't matter what industry you're in. It doesn't matter whether you're in aerospace or accounting. Clients and customers all have their own special needs. It's up to you to find their needs and prove we can meet them.

ARE WE OFF BALANCE?

How many companies do you know that have good products and pour more and more effort into product development? Yet when it comes to putting effort into improving their sales capability, they don't think about giving it the same emphasis.

While I was writing this book, I was interviewed on the Brian Hayes show on LBC Radio. Brian asked me if I thought companies were allocating too much effort to production and not enough to marketing.

"Is there a guideline on the way companies should break down their resources--a percentage that should be spent on each?" Brian asked.

What I told the listeners is that production oriented companies often put more energy into production and less into marketing. Isn't this natural? We all continue to do more of what we do best. Yet, we have to get the balance right or we run the danger of becoming lopsided.

If you're running a production-oriented company, you may want to sit back and take a look at it. Is the balance right?

Could you get more profit by increasing your attention to marketing? Chances are, yes. Most companies can.

Think what results could be achieved with the right emphasis--with everyone trained to know more facts. With knowledge of more product features, they would appeal to a wider range of customers. Like the appliance saleswoman, their customer base would thrive while the competitors, with less sales competence, would fall by the wayside.

IDENTIFY THE OBSTACLES

What are some of the obstacles that stand in the way of getting people trained to know more product features, to know the facts inside, outside and upside down? To become high achievers and to help us pursue profit with vigor?

It won't be an easy road ahead. If you hope it will be, you might as well be content with your current profits. It sounds easy to get people to learn about their product, but it isn't. If it was, people like the appliance saleswoman would not be scarce. But she is.

If you're going to *pursue profit* you have to be a realist and you have to attack obstacles head on. The truth is that salespeople can't always be expected to learn all the product features without some form of training--without support from management.

Why? Perhaps because the product is complex and requires explanation. Perhaps it's simple, but the uses of it vary widely. Or perhaps, as we said earlier, salespeople may not have considered how important product knowledge is to selling. In that case, you'll have to motivate them. Knowing the features is fundamental to sales--it's the foundation, the base of your pyramid, on which everything else will stand. When you or your people have become authorities like the appliance saleswoman--then your job will be complete. Congratulations--you will have done it!

WHAT SYSTEMS WILL YOU USE?

Now, what system will you use to drill these product features into the minds of everyone? Who will do the drilling? I once worked for a company that wouldn't let the salespeople talk to the service people. But the salespeople were new and the service people were the only ones who knew about the product. The sales manager was told to do the training, but he was new too and didn't know any more than the salespeople.

Since we were all hired as seasoned salespeople, we knew the fundamentals of selling. We were experts at getting appointments, setting targets, and analyzing the prospective customer base. We were eager to move. But, we didn't know very much about the product. Sound silly? Yes, but it's true, and it happens more often than you think.

Why hire someone and not give him or her the tools they need to do the job? You're *pursuing profit*, so you won't make this mistake--you'll give them the tools.

But in devising your effective system for drilling, you'll hit obstacles. What will yours be? Time? Attitude of others? Your own motivation? Money? Lack of ideas? Lack of personnel to organize or carry out the training? You might as well look at your obstacles now, because wanting something is not enough. You'll have to overcome the obstacles.

My good friend Walter Blackburn of PeopleTrack, has an effective approach to obstacles. He believes that if we are to achieve our goals, we have to look carefully at things that could hold us back., "If we identify obstacles in our path and plan ways to overcome them, our chances of success are greater," Walter says. Think about that as it relates to training.

Another trainer I know also looks at obstacles. In his workshops on developing power to get things done, he draws the comparison between obstacles and roadblocks. We can choose to stop at a roadblock, never reaching our goal, or we can take a detour. To take a detour we simply go over, around, or through the obstacle. By knowing there will be obstacles, we can mentally prepare to take the detours.

If Bill Sykes and I believed in obstacles, we wouldn't have written this book. It would be easy to let time and other obstacles stand in our way. How could we take the time out to write and still both run our own businesses? How would we communicate our ideas, with the Atlantic between us? And so it goes, obstacles always loom, as they will for you as you bring sales performance to its peak. You'll need to devote time and perhaps money to training and you'll need to engender motivation.

GET THEIR SUPPORT

Let's say you've decided it's necessary to make yourself or your people better 'product knowledge experts.' You've overcome the obstacles of time by deciding to set aside a certain period each day or week until the learning curve is up. Or, perhaps you give yourself or others material to learn each day, and then test for understanding.

How will you get their support on it? That's a challenging obstacle to overcome. You'll probably have to use the technique Dr. Lyle used to get people to stop smoking. He let them see incentives for not smoking. You can give people incentives by linking their goals to the new training.

I like the illustration Peggy Lindsay used at Henley Staff College relating to employee motivation. She showed a wide arrow going diagonally across a page, pointing to the upper right hand corner. This represents the employee's goal. The company goals are represented by another wide arrow going diagonally across the page in the other direction, pointing to the upper left-hand corner. The area where the two arrows overlap is the area of common goal. What do you as the company, and each of your people have as common goals? When you identify this, you'll have your motivators.

Surely a common goal is to create more sales, especially if you or your people work on commission. But even then, remember that not all people are motivated by money.

What else will product knowledge do for the individual? Perhaps they'll get more job satisfaction, meet more people, get recognition, experience adventure. Whatever they seek, it's up to us as managers to find out and link their goals to our training. It's not easy. It takes time and effort to get to know people. Peggy Lindsay's system helps us to visualize the overlap of employee and employer goals, and to concentrate our energy at that overlap area.

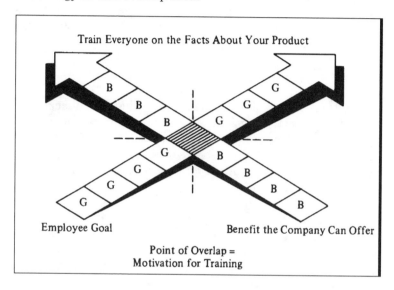

Train Everyone on the Facts About Your Product

Employee Goal   Benefit the Company Can Offer

Point of Overlap =
Motivation for Training

MAKE LEARNING EASY

Obviously you'll want to make learning as easy as possible if you want to make your people authorities on your product.

Tony Buzan, Edward DeBono, and others have done interesting studies on the brain to see what techniques make us learn and remember. Since 80% of what we hear is forgotten after two days, your training system will have to include repetition of material, and repetitive testing.

REPEAT, REPEAT, REPEAT

The British Broadcasting Corporation, well known worldwide for its excellent productions, ran a German course in conjunction with adult schools that I attended while living in England. Anyone could enroll in their local school for the normal course with the instructor. In addition, the BBC ran supplemental material for the course four times per week, twice on television and twice on the radio. Those of us learning German could get five repeats each week to reinforce our learning. It was a fabulous system, and all students agreed they learned faster by having the repetitive broadcasts. Therefore, if you want people to remember material, create several ways and varieties of repetition.

GIVE IMMEDIATE FEEDBACK

Another aspect of learning is immediate feedback. The brain learns best when it receives answers to test questions immediately. The answers reinforce the learning process. I had a teacher at school I respected above all others. He knew more about learning, motivation, and human needs than any I had in all the years of my education.

Mr. Wisely taught algebra to 150 of us each year in Glendale, California, and knew the importance of getting immediate reinforcement to the learning process. He devised a self-grading system for correcting the exam papers immediately after the test. By having the results the same day while the material was fresh in our minds, we learned faster.

Did you ever have an exam at school one week, then get the answers the next week? By the time the answers came, you'd undoubtedly forgotten the questions. So give people instant feedback whenever you can.

GIVE POSITIVE, NOT NEGATIVE, FEEDBACK

What about the learning environment? Your job is to make people learn quickly, not to embarrass them in front of their colleagues. Some people learn more slowly than others. Some people need to ask more questions than others. Bill Sykes's background in organizational development has taught him to be sensitive to people's egos. At our seminars, he often warns, "Don't embarrass people publicly, even in jest. The person you're embarrassing won't like it and neither will the rest of the group. They'll side with the one being embarrassed, not you."

The other side of the coin is positive reinforcement. We all learn faster and reach higher performance with positive reinforcement--a kind word of encouragement here and there goes a long way.

That ingenious math teacher, Mr. Wisely, used to write short notes on our homework papers. When we got a difficult problem right, he marked GREAT or EXCELLENT next to the problem. Imagine how good we felt each time we got the paper back.

When we got it wrong he said, *"You were on the right track until this point."* Did we feel deflated? Certainly not. We knew we were on the right track. Mr. Wisely said so; he encouraged us. He didn't say, "You went wrong here." There's a big difference, *one is positive, one is negative.*

Are we any different when we're 40 than when we're 14? No, we all need positive encouragement. I worked hard in Mr. Wisely's class and did better than in any other class. Don't we want that dedication and high performance from our people when we *pursue profit*? Why not give a little encouragement like Mr. Wisely did? It doesn't take long and it gets big results.

REDUCE RIDICULE AND JUDGEMENT

I remember the woman who taught me to sew. She was a master of motivation for achieving perfection. When we did something wrong, she didn't ridicule us. She simply said, *"This* has got to go." The emphasis was on the word 'this,' not on us. When we did it right, she examined it carefully and praised us for doing the job well. Somehow we all ended up doing our best for Dorothy Kearns.

Think about it. Can you change your wording to remove negativity and judgment? If you do, you'll be amazed at the results, both in terms of personal relationships and motivating others.

Charles Schwab, who back in the 1920's was paid over a million dollars a year for his ability to manage people, said that people work better and give greater effort under a spirit of approval than they ever do under a spirit of criticism! He said, "There is nothing that so kills the ambitions of a person as criticism ... I never criticize anyone."

Isn't this good advice for you and me in motivating our people? Most people learn and thrive in a supportive environment. When managers learn to increase their supportiveness, giving each person specific positive feedback, they get an overwhelming increase in results. The same is true of parents with children, and vice versa. After all, aren't we all managers when it comes to human relationships?

GET COMPETITIVE

What else motivates people to learn? Most salespeople like competitiveness. A little competition could spark up your training. That algebra teacher, who knew so well how to motivate, had another effective gimmick. He used to reassign seats after each exam according to the score each person achieved. The first row on the left had the highest achievers. Imagine it. It wasn't just an Honor Roll posted on a bulletin board in some obscure corner. No, there was a physical recognition of the high achievers there for all to see.

As we 'winners' sat in the seats of that first row, do you think we absorbed that feeling of success?

Do you think we wanted to let it go? No, we were determined to keep it and we tried harder each week. So did the others; they tried to overtake one another, and before long the standard of the whole group went up. We were untouchable. No one in the school could match the standards of Mr. Wisely's students.

Do we want our people to be unbeatable? Let's give them competition and recognition. Do you know who in your group knows more product features than anyone else? Find out. Acknowledge them. Give the others a standard to beat.

Sound gimmicky, childish? Of course it does, but it works because there's a little bit of kid in all of us. And a little competitiveness. Why not work with human nature, not against it. It makes sense.

The next time someone reproaches you for using gimmicky methods of competition, remind them about human nature. And let them see the results before they condemn. You'll have the winning team, not them.

SET A HIGH STANDARD

What about this concept of product knowledge training? We know it will improve their performance, but isn't it awkward to suddenly bring in a new training philosophy?

Do we really have the right to impose rigid learning practices on our people? The answer is yes, emphatically yes. They love it--or learn to.

Think about the international accounting and consulting firms that fly their trainees to the worldwide headquarters for three weeks of solid, hard indoctrination. They train and test seven days a week, from morning until night. The evening and weekend sessions are optional but anybody missing them will probably not pass the rigid exams along the way.

This is good preparation for the dedication to the job that the consultants give to their companies after the training. I know several people who work for these firms now, and it would be hard to find better trained, more dedicated employees than these. And their customers appreciate it.

Wouldn't we all like to instill this dedication in our people? Why not start with a good solid training system and set a high standard for everyone to live up to?

I remember Dale Carnegie training, one of the most beneficial courses I attended early in my career. One principle was to give people a reputation to live up to. If we set a high standard, people do rise to the occasion. Best of all, they feel good about themselves. We can look to other success stories—big and small--they all devote substantial time to training.

And employees expect to burn a little midnight oil in doing their job and in learning, if the pressure from management says it's necessary. If we set a high standard for our people by expecting them to become authorities on the product, it will set the scene for them to become high achievers in other facets of sales.

Bill Sykes tells the story of Michael, a colleague who once worked for Parker Pen. One day Michael had the opportunity to drive through his town with Mr. Parker, who pointed out every jewelry and stationery store asking if that store stocked their pens. But Mr. Parker didn't stop there. He expected his employees to know every aspect of their business: which inks were purchased, what typewriters, what percentage of the business they had, whether or not they did their own service, and so on.

Mr. Parker didn't settle for second best. He expected his people to know everything, not just product features, but anything and everything about the customer. If we're in *pursuit of profit*, shouldn't we expect the same?

BE INVENTIVE

Perhaps you're in need of ideas for training in order to make your people authorities on your product or service. If so, why not be inventive? In one company I worked for, I went out to interview satisfied customers about how they used our product. I made this part of my training exercise.

Then I wrote the results of the interviews as training case studies. Then, combined with photographs, the success stories were used as press releases and promotions.

While doing the interviews, I discovered new facts about the products and got quotes from the customers that we used later in selling. We understood the customers better and our enthusiasm grew.

Was it a long process? No. The whole exercise of setting up the interview, carrying it out, and writing it up took less than a day of time for each case study.

And here's the best part. New business resulted from two out of the six companies interviewed. The customers had their interest heightened during the interview and placed new orders with our company. That was an unexpected fringe benefit. It proves what can be done when we use imagination in developing methods that train and motivate our people.

What imaginative learning exercise would work in your business? Don't discount any new idea until you've given it a chance. Einstein said, "Imagination is more important than intelligence." Let's not be so intellectual and traditional that we fail to be imaginative. Let's upgrade our sales skills through every source possible.

Remember this fundamental fact about sales:

Train yourself and others to become product experts.

ACTION SHEET
Chapter 2

Ideas for Development:

1. Remember that you'll lose credibility with customers if you don't have the facts about your product or service.
2. Ask yourself if the balance is right between attention to production and attention to sales and marketing.
3. Identify the obstacles to product knowledge training.
4. Be creative in training yourself and others, and make it easy and beneficial.
5. Give positive reinforcement, get competitive and set a high standard.
6. List other points here:
7.
8.

Of the above ideas, which one is likely to yield the best results?

What percentage of sales (or performance) increase could realistically be expected?

How long would it take: to develop the idea? to get results?

Who would have to be involved?

What date should we start?

What is the first step I should take?

Chapter 3

Bring Your Benefits
Into the Open

"Eat your vegetables, they're full of vitamins," said little Johnny's parents to Johnny. But little Johnny didn't know what vitamins were. He didn't see what good they would be to him. Neither did the buyer of the fax machine when the salesman told him, "It uses the latest high-speed digital transmission technology."

"Oh?" said the buyer. He was as confused as little Johnny. He knew about as much about high speed digital technology as Johnny knew about vitamins--and cared less. What would that do for him? He only wanted to send copies of contracts from his office in London to his colleagues in Australia.

REMEMBER THAT PEOPLE BUY
ONLY THE BENEFITS, NOT THE FEATURES

Then the salesman went on to say, "This means you can send and receive copies at the speed of a phone call--in fact, in 28 seconds."

"Whew, now we're getting somewhere," thought the buyer. I'll take one.

The salesman finally told him the benefit he would derive from digital technology. The benefit met his needs, so he bought. People don't buy the features of our products and services, they buy the benefits.

Not long ago a client of ours from Britain, dealing with laboratory equipment, came to the US to sell his product. He had superb products with many technical features. What did he do when he got in front of the buyer? He did what most people do. He fell into the trap of telling the buyer all the features, but didn't explain the benefits.

Luckily, Bill was there with him and brought him to a halt. "Wait a minute, Peter. Could you back up over that brown etched line on the thermometer? Why is that important?" asked Bill.

"Oh, well, most of our competitors have painted lines. Those are less precise than ours. With our etched line you get a more accurate reading."

The buyer's eyes lit up. "A more accurate reading. Oh, that's very interesting," said the buyer. Previously, while our client had talked about the brown etched line, the buyer had been nodding in agreement but obviously hadn't recognized the benefit.

Why should he? After all, he dealt with hundreds of suppliers. He had a catalogue of 30,000 different pieces of equipment. He couldn't be expected to know the benefits of them all. Why should any buyer, for that matter, recognize the benefits if we don't tell them what they are? People are no different than little Johnny, or the fax machine buyer. They don't know unless we tell them. And they won't buy unless they recognize the benefit. Remember this the next time you want to convince anybody of anything!

IDENTIFY A BENEFIT FOR
EVERY FEATURE OF YOUR PRODUCT OR SERVICE

In our sales development seminar, Bill and I throw the attendees straight into an exercise on benefits. They're asked to bring information about one particular product or service so that it can act as the base of their activity throughout the course. Their first task is to circulate around the room and tell each of the other attendees the benefits of their own product. They have 60 seconds to tell each person, then rotate to the next.

Can you guess what happens? They soon start falling into the trap that our client Peter and most people fall into. They describe the features, not the benefits. In fact, they often have difficulty at first trying to decide what the benefits are for each product. But we don't despair.

With thought and practice, people become proficient at identifying the benefits of the product. Then they can start applying their knowledge to increase their sales. The results can be dramatic. From this exercise alone, we have people, who come to the seminars from around the world, write to tell us later that they got a 30% and higher increase in sales just from stressing the benefits. Think about how you can put a push on benefits in your own business.

TALK, WRITE AND THINK BENEFITS

Benefits should be used in all of the following areas:

1. Sales presentations
2. Literature
3. Advertising
4. Contracts and proposals
5. Letters
6. Getting appointments
7. In management meetings to make our point
8. In public speaking to make our point
9. In personal life to make our point

Some people are naturals when it comes to talking about benefits. One client, Laurence, was telling me not long ago about the machinery his company had developed for label making. "This machine cuts raw material costs by 25%," he said. "Any company overseas should be delighted to work with us on a licensing basis. Think of the money we can save them!"

No wonder he has been able to lead his company to a prominent position. He knows people want to hear benefits and he goes straight to them. Did you hear him talk about features? Did he say, "Our machine has the technology to coat the release paper in-line while it's producing the labels?" No, he skipped the feature altogether.

He went straight to the benefit. If we want to talk about the features, we can do that later. First let's talk about the benefit. Everyone understands that. Let's capture their interest with the benefit and move on to features later.

Can your people talk, write, and think benefits? Perhaps they don't have his know-how. Most people don't. But with practice everyone can improve.

If we can get benefits ingrained in the minds of everyone, think of the results we can achieve. Let's look closer to gain a better understanding...

ELIMINATE THE BENEFIT ROADBLOCKS

What holds people back from either recognizing or discussing the benefits? Obviously they have to know what they are before they can use them in selling. In looking closely at this problem, we see that there are three things standing in the way:

1. Thinking that benefits are obvious.
2. Confusing the benefit with the feature.
3. Fear of being personal.

DON'T THINK THAT BENEFITS ARE OBVIOUS

First, they are often so close to a product that they think the benefit is obvious to the buyer. So they don't bring it out into the open.

Of course, it's never as obvious to the buyer as it is to those of us who work with the product day in and day out. Did Laurence think the "technology to coat the release paper in-line would be obvious to us?" No. But a technician who works closely with the machinery might think it was obvious because he's so close to it.

If we're in *pursuit of profit*, we must get our people to ignore what seems obvious to them. They must talk benefits first. Let features follow.

DON'T CONFUSE THE BENEFIT WITH THE FEATURE

The second thing holding people back from recognizing the benefits of their products or services is that they get confused about the difference between features and benefits. For the fax machine salesman, it's easy to see that the latest high speed digital transmission technology is the feature. What's the benefit? "You get copies fast."

But some people would be tempted to say, "The machine works fast." They would falsely think of that as the benefit. But it's not. 'The machine works fast' still describes the machine just as 'high speed technology' describes the machine. But 'you get fast copies' describes what the customer gets.

When we tell what the customer gets, we're talking benefits.

One seminar attendee was enthusiastic about benefits that he wanted to present his own benefits to the group. We gave him two minutes to come up and tell us. For the first minute and a half he talked about the wiring configuration inside his telecommunications product. I stopped him and said, "Bob, when do we get to hear what the customer gets? You only have 30 seconds left." He said, "I can't tell you the benefits until you understand how it worked." He had missed the point.

We then asked him more about the customer's needs until he was able to state the benefits they receive in a simple way, forgetting the complex wiring. "Oh," he said in astonishment, "now I think I know why no one at work understands me when I give demonstrations. Now I know I have to talk about what people get, not how it works! Thanks."

He suddenly realized the great advantage he would have in communication by talking about the benefits the user receives first. This puts everyone in the picture. Then, when the scene is set, he can talk about features.

The third thing holding people back from discussing benefits is their fear of being too personal or too direct.

And, since benefits do relate to people, this is a legitimate concern. But there are ways to overcome it. We don't have to hit the buyer over the head with it. We don't have to say, "Since you're so overweight, this dieting class will be good for you." What we can do is to use a third party reference. We can say "John Jones came to the slimming class at the beginning of last month, and he's already made great progress. He's playing tennis now, which he's always wanted to do. Everyone who comes regularly to the class benefits." This eliminates being too personal and whets the buyer's appetite for the benefits.

This reference to another person is very effective. Remember it regardless of what you're selling. Use it and your sales will skyrocket.

USE BENEFITS IN ALL ASPECTS OF LIFE

Remember the third party reference in personal life too. The next time you want to convince your daughter or son or wife or husband or anyone in your life to do something, think of the benefit and then tell them about it. Tell the story as it benefits someone else. It will whet their appetite and motivate action.

Talk about benefits in your literature, in your advertising, and in the letters you write every day. Talk about benefits at management meetings, and the next time you speak to a group. It will work wonders. Use it to benefit your community.

USE BENEFITS TO GET RESULTS
IN THE COMMUNITY TOO

What if you want your Rotary group to accept 'Guide Dogs for the Blind' for their charity, as Mic Bryant, a friend of mine in England, did? Perhaps you can tell them a moving story about how someone you know benefited from having a guide dog.

Let them know the feeling of community pride they themselves will gain from supporting this cause. Capture their hearts and minds. Perhaps you'll be as successful as Mic was. His group went on to present the results of their charity to the Guide Dogs for the Blind Association at the House of Commons in London. Think what more we can accomplish for society when we help others to focus on benefits.

INFLUENCE OPINIONS

Do you ever need to influence the opinions of an audience? The founder of Sony Corporation of Japan knows how to use benefits to convince. I saw him hold an audience of 4500 people spellbound at the Albert Hall, at the Institute of Directors Convention, when he discussed the future of robotics. Would robots endanger the work force? Mr. Akio Morita likened the advent of robotics to the advance of computers.

He reminded us of the benefits of the computer industry and the jobs created. He focused our minds on the benefits of job creation when new technology emerges. As he spoke in English while referring to his notes in Japanese, he awed us with his ability to sway opinion. He stressed benefits in order to make his point--benefits everyone could relate to.

No wonder this man has brought his company into a leading world position. If he can use benefits to sway a group of over four thousand people in a language not native to him, think what we can do in our own companies and our own community. Let's start at home, like Mic Bryant did, to help the community. Let's improve our business by stressing benefits now, and watch the results we get.

Remember this fundamental fact of sales:

Talk benefits first, second, and third.
Talk features later.

ACTION SHEET
Chapter 3

Ideas for Development:

1. Identify a benefit for *every* feature of your product or service.
2. Increase sales by adding benefits to brochures, letters, proposals and all written material.
3. Increase personal effectiveness by talking about the benefits of your ideas to your listener in business and personal life.
4. Never assume that the benefits are obvious to your listener – they are not.
5. Don't confuse the feature with the benefit.
6. Use benefits to get results in the community and to influence opinions.
7. List other points here:
8.

Of the above ideas, which one is likely to yield the best results?

What percentage of sales (or performance) increase could realistically be expected?

How long would it take: to develop the idea? to get results?

Who would have to be involved?

What date should we start?

What is the first step I should take?

PART 2

THE PERFECT WAY TO MOTIVATE

Chapter 4

Remember This and You Will Succeed

In one of my speeches on how to motivate, a woman came up to me afterwards and said, "Oh, Christine. I realize now what I've been doing wrong with my husband. He's been trying to start a new business and every night when he comes home, I tell him everything I think he's done wrong. No wonder he's discouraged. Now I see from your talk that I have to tell him what he's done right!"

The same is true in business. As managers, it's tempting to tell people what they've done wrong and not acknowledge what's right. I often address business groups and tell them to start blowing the whistle on good performance instead of bad. The results will amaze you.

I addressed the Sony Corporation with the importance of positive reinforcement and afterwards the Director in charge had silver plated whistles made for his managers. He sent me a copy of the letter that went with it saying "Here's a reminder following Christine Harvey's message to blow the whistle for employees with admirable performances."

I often start my speeches by asking the audience to consider how many teachers they ever had who really, really motivated them. The answer is usually one to three. Then I ask how many bosses they've had who really motivate them. The answer is usually one or two. So few motivators.

If you think of the people who motivated you, you may discover that it was someone who showed you the best in yourself – someone who gave you faith in yourself..

What if you were to do that for others? What would the benefit be to you?

Perhaps the answer is in this slogan I've created. "Show people the best in themselves and they will follow you anywhere." Think of how loyalty from colleagues will impact your career. Think of how loyalty from customers will impact you. And think about how loyalty from family and friends will impact you. Yes, showing people the best in themselves – giving them positive feedback, makes all the difference in the world.

Secondly, when you motivate people, the job gets done quickly and effectively. How often have you gone to meetings in which people agree to do things. Later you discover nothing was done. Often it's because they weren't motivated.

MOTIVATE YOURSELF AND OTHERS THROUGH POSITIVE REINFORCEMENT

Positive reinforcement can be used in your own life to motivate yourself too. In my book, Secrets of the World's Top Sales Performers, I quote Michael Renz who uses positive reinforcement daily. He mentally goes through the day and discovers anything that went wrong. Then he determines how to fix it and make sure it doesn't happen again. Then he thinks of his successes. He said to me, "Christine, if I carry negativity into my day, I'm not doing the right job for myself or my company. It's important that I keep my self esteem up."

I was addressing a group in Monte Carlo once. There were about 350 of them, mainly company directors from Scandinavia.

After explaining the concept of positive reinforcement, I asked them to think of one person they'd most like to motivate. Then I asked them to imagine using the phone to call that person and use this three-part process:

26. Tell the person what they did right.
27. Tell the person how that action benefited the company.
28. Thank the person.

After my speech, there was another speaker. He was a member of the European Parliament who spoke for about 40 minutes then we all went into the ballroom for lunch.

I was only seated for a matter of minutes, when I had a tap on the shoulder. I looked around and saw a very exuberant man.

"Mrs. Harvey, " he said with a voice full of emotion. What a close call I had!" He explained that he telephoned one of his most valued salesmen and told him how much he appreciated him using the three-part process I had described in my speech. "John," he said, "Do you remember last year when you gave up your weekend to help the company move so we could be operational the following Monday? Well, we gained a customer that Monday who now accounts for 10% of our business. John without your dedication, we would not have been open and would have lost that important customer. Thanks, John."

Then he went on to tell me John's reaction. John confided in him that he had not been feeling very appreciated recently and had gone out job hunting. He had another offer and was planning to turn in his resignation the next day! "But because you cared enough to pick up the phone and call me all the way from Monte Carlo, I'm really touched. I'll reconsider my resignation," the valued employee said.

You can never underestimate the importance of positive reinforcement.

Use it with employees, use it with customers,   use it with yourself and your family. Undoubtedly you have goals you want to reach, and here's the perfect place to use positive reinforcement.

AGREE ON GOALS

Are we leaving motivation to chance? Do we give lip service to motivation, but let the employees go in all directions unnoticed? Do we sometimes acknowledge them and sometimes not, leading to confusion, then blame them for being unpredictable? Do we even know what the end goal is, or do we wait until people go in the wrong direction and then lambaste them for not finding their own way to the undetermined goal? In reality, many of us are trying to motivate people in our business and personal life without giving them direction.

Do people tell their spouses what they really want from them to help each other make their lives together a success? Or do they let their spouses guess at it for 20 years and then, when they're wrong, divorce them?

Do we talk with our colleagues and employees to find out what their goals in life are, and then plan a path that meets both the company's and the employee's objectives? If so, then everyone profits.

Those experts in motivational psychology who say that a person's happiness is directly proportional to the speed at which they are moving towards their goal make an interesting point. If we can keep people moving toward goals, we keep the level of satisfaction up. We keep a positive cycle going.

BE SPECIFIC IN YOUR FEEDBACK

Let's imagine we have a path with five points along it leading to the end results. When our subjects get to the right point we want to tell them they've arrived. We don't want to say, "You're about there." Otherwise, they'll keep looking for the exact point.

Yet, as managers, people often think vague acknowledgment is reinforcement. They haven't learned that exact, specific feedback is necessary to get the subject to the end goal in the shortest possible time. They think a smile, a nod, or even the lack of punishment is enough to keep people on course!

Instead, we must tell them exactly what they did that was correct. "Nice job, John," may be a good start, but it's not specific. If you want to give reinforcement that gets results, you'll include exactly what was done and what effect it had. "John, That section of the proposal on pricing was a masterpiece. The numbers were laid out in a format that was concise and easy to read. Thanks John! If we win the bid, it's due to your excellent contribution."

You can use positive reinforcement with colleagues too. In a training seminar, Bill and I might say to each other, "I really liked the way you involved the participants in the second session by relating the material to their industries and to them personally. I noticed that those particular people took a stronger leadership role later on." You can use positive reinforcement in selling too. One top performer uses it like this. "Mr. Jones, you told me that your objective was this, this and this. Now you've gone through and made your selections. If you go down the list of your choices one by one, you'll see you've achieved this, this and this. Those were excellent choices. Congratulations." In this way, sales stay closed!

It's important to be specific. Financial people relate well to the importance of specifics. They wouldn't dream of working with figures "vaguely in the range of such and such," so why should we work with vague feedback. It simply doesn't tell anybody anything.

Positive feedback has lasting results. It's the perfect way to motivate.

Remember the perfect way to motivate is to:

Give Positive Reinforcement

ACTION SHEET
Chapter 4

Ideas for Development:

1. Give positive reinforcement to people to achieve results and loyalty.
2. Use positive reinforcement to motivate yourself and others.
3. Use positive reinforcement to retain good employees.
4. Use positive reinforcement in your personal life.
5. Agree on goals and give positive reinforcement at every stage of progress.
6. List other points here:
7
8.

Of the above ideas, which one is likely to yield the best results?

What percentage of sales (or performance) increase could realistically be expected?

How long would it take: to develop the idea? to get results?

Who would have to be involved?

What date should we start?

What is the first step I should take?

Chapter 5

Leadership Is for Everyone

Do we need good performance? The Japanese think so. I remember well a conversation I had with a business acquaintance in Tokyo.

"You know, Christine," he said, "we have a commitment here that Westerners don't understand. People take their careers and their responsibilities seriously here. Perhaps you could say too seriously."

"I'll tell you the truth. If a manager of a major company is given a very important job--let's say to develop a new machine cheaper and better than the rival competitor--then the success in this job means a major promotion. Failure means demotion. I guarantee that the person will do everything possible to succeed on time, within budget."

"And what if the person fails?" I asked. "Well now," he said, "that person may well commit suicide. That is the seriousness of commitments."

As I sat in the palatial surrounding of the hotel in Tokyo, I thought about commitment. Yes, my friend was right, that is a commitment Westerners don't understand. But if we were in that environment long enough, or were born into it, we would understand it. We would live by it.

Tell Them What's Expected

The same is true of breeding leadership. If you set the right environment for people, they develop leadership. If you set a lax environment, they develop laxness.

If we want our people to learn commitment and leadership, we have to make sure they know:

1. The end results expected.
2. How to segment and handle the task.

Bill Sykes remembers well the practices of his first boss, Piers Flashman, at Horlicks Pharmaceuticals Company. Piers was one of the early influences on Bill because his management style was so effective.

Piers always took time with his employees in delegating responsibility. He didn't assume that they knew what the end goal was. He took time to make sure the job objective was clearly laid out.

Bill remembers when they were faced with a massive job of setting up a new pharmaceutical research laboratory. This required purchasing equipment, moving people, and so on. Piers would explain, "Now I'm taking responsibility for the building contract, and I want you to be responsible for sales administration," and so on.

Regardless of the pressure he was under, he would stop at the end of the day to make sure everyone understood their responsibilities.

Bill and his colleagues who were just out of college thrived under this leadership. People must know where they're going in order to have commitment getting there.

Bill, in his organizational development work, sees examples often within companies of managers presuming employees know how to handle a task and know what end result is expected. They don't. Usually they don't see what is obvious to do until we show them.

What ability must we develop in people if they are to assume responsibility and leadership? It's the ability not just to take action, but to get the end goal accomplished.

If you ask your employee to get information about opening a bank account, you don't mean you want some information. You mean you want all the information necessary to open the account. Most employees who eventually fail in leadership think their job is finished when they get whatever information the bank gives them. They don't stop to question whether the information meets the end goal. They don't ask, "Do I now have the complete information necessary to open the account?"

Many think their job is done because they were told to call the bank and they did. They tried to get information. They got information. But they didn't take it to the logical conclusion. That gap between the task and the results, is the leadership gap. Our job is to train people to see the end result and all the segments necessary to reach it.

TEACH THE DIFFERENCE BETWEEN TRYING AND DOING

Why? Because when we have everyone reaching the end result and not just working on the task, our companies will profit. How can people be taught to bridge that gap?

First we have to make people aware of the leadership gap the difference between just trying and accomplishing.

A psychologist I know uses a very powerful technique to demonstrate this difference. She starts by throwing a pencil on the floor. Then she says, "Try to pick up that pencil." As people bend over and almost touch it, she says, "Wait, I said try to pick it up, not pick it up."

Do you see the meaning of try? We either do it or we don't. Trying and accomplishing are two different things.

I remember an employee who called the bank for me. I wanted to invest some company money for a short period of time and needed to know the interest rate and the withdrawal restrictions. There is an overnight call account and a two-day notice account. We needed details on both US dollars and Japanese yen.

The employee called the bank. The bank manager was in a meeting and the foreign exchange expert's line was busy. A second call revealed that the bank manager knew some answers, but not all of them, and would have his expert get all the details. A third call revealed that the expert knew the interest rate, but was unclear about the withdrawal terms.

That went on and on. Until I made my employee realize that their job was actually to *get* all the information, not just *try* to get it. They then probed until they got all the answers they needed. That's the value of a leader--one who can be counted on to accomplish--not just to try.

TACKLE EVEN SMALL TASKS RELENTLESSLY

If a person can be trained to tackle a task like the one above relentlessly, they will learn to handle bigger management problems the same way.

Just as Bill's first boss knew, people have to understand the expected end result if they are to develop leadership. By holding people responsible for small complete tasks, we are nurturing leadership for the future.

How do we foster this leadership, and commitment to high standards? As managers, we have to start with ourselves.

I remember a hit song that said, "You've got to stand for something, or you're going to fall for anything."

We have to be known for a motto that says trying isn't enough. When people see your standards, they recognize you as a leader. They follow in your footsteps. Thus we help people bridge the leadership gap.

One of my past employees was never afraid to ask questions or contribute her opinions, and they are always valued opinions. When given a task, she always probed to get all the details. She always made sure she knew the expected end results.

When I asked her about it she told me, "I always feel it's better to stand up and make a decision and have it be wrong, than not to make a decision at all." That's the way she felt people could progress and not stagnate.

If everyone took this attitude, our companies would prosper from a wealth of new ideas and improvements. Yet fear often stands in their way.

It's up to people to overcome their fear, realizing it will help their progress. It's also up to managers to create a safe environment for this to happen.

When we take on a new job, like fostering leadership, we face uncertainties. We open up new horizons. We grow. Our leadership ability grows. People then rely on us as leaders. It's then that we get results second to none.

Remember the perfect way to motivate is to:

Bring out the leadership in everyone.

ACTION SHEET
Chapter 5

Ideas for Development:

1. Set an example of commitment and leadership
2. Let the expected end result be known.
3. Make sure people know how to segment tasks.
4. Teach the differences between trying and doing.
5. Create a safe and open environment for ideas.
6. List other points here:
7
8.

Of the above ideas, which one is likely to yield the best results?

What percentage of sales (or performance) increase could realistically be expected?

How long would it take: to develop the idea? to get results?

Who would have to be involved?

What date should we start?

What is the first step I should take?

PART 3

Basic Techniques To Make Buying Easy

Chapter 6

Help the Customers Recognize Their Needs

Let's examine some basic techniques to make buying easy for your customers. Here's in example. Imagine that executives are transferred and, as consumers, they have to buy a home and start furnishing it. They have to buy things for every room. They're under pressure and they're in a new town. They don't know quite what to buy or where to find everything. But it must be finished in two weeks and ready to live in.

In most businesses, including highly technical businesses, our customers are similar to the customers above. They need to accomplish something under time pressure. They don't know quite what's available to meet their requirements, but they must solve their problem soon.

GET THE CUSTOMER TO VERBALIZE NEEDS

Perhaps the consumers haven't had time to examine every aspect of their needs. They know only that they need to have the house furnished. They may not, under time pressure, decide on the exact size and shape of the furniture until they see what's available. Smart salespeople will help them analyze their needs. They will then suggest ways they can help--ways their furniture will fit the consumers' needs.

A salesperson might ask, "Do you want a casual or a formal atmosphere?" "Are your rooms large or small?" "Do you need it now, or can you wait for delivery?" The smart salespeople will ask questions and get the customers to verbalize their needs.

MARKING THE BRAIN CELLS

There must be something in our brains that acts like a rubber stamp. When prospective customers verbalize a need, it becomes indelibly stamped on their brain. It's true in all businesses. If customers don't state their needs, often they aren't quite clear about what their needs are. By asking questions we help them to put their needs into focus.

Often, because prospects don't know everything that's on the market, they express their needs broadly rather than specifically. We often have prospective clients coming into our office for an initial consultation who tell us that they want to increase sales. That's good as a broad base, but we need to use the questioning process to get them to identify specific needs. We might ask which markets they now deal in, or which they would like to enter or do better in.

Every business has its own needs, and we can get customers to recognize those needs by asking the right questions. Questioning is essential. Prospects who are told exactly what a product does, its benefits and why they should buy it are not yet being convinced. However when they are asked questions about their needs, their answers reinforce their reason for buying. They become involved in the buying process.

BECOME A FACILITATOR WITH PROBING QUESTIONS

Most prospects are happy to be asked questions about their needs. In fact, they are pleased that someone cares enough about their problems to ask and to listen. It helps to build an atmosphere in which the prospects feel they are buying rather than being sold to. No one in sales should be afraid to ask questions because most people appreciate it.

To put yourself in the frame of mind to ask questions effectively, think of yourself as a buying facilitator, not a seller. Or think of yourself as a consultant diagnosing the problem and proposing alternatives. Your goal is to have the prospects feel you're on their side, helping them to get the outcome which suits them best.

Recognize the Need or Lose the Sale

Occasionally people resist the questioning process. But they can be persuaded to see the value of the questioning line in two ways:
- By explaining your reasons for questions
- By asking their permission

We find it useful, after initial ice breaking, to start the meeting by saying something like this: "Mr. Smith, since there's not enough time today for you to tell us everything about your company, nor for us to tell you everything about ours, perhaps we could start by giving you an overview of our service." Then you'll be in a better position to tell us your needs as they relate to these. By the end of the meeting we should be able to see whether there is an area of mutual interest. If there is, then we can tell you about our service in detail. Would that be OK?

If we tried to tell them all our services from beginning to end, or listened to their company history without guiding them to their needs through the questioning process, their needs would never be clarified. They would leave in despair. The questioning process keeps the discussion on track because every question is designed to bring both sides closer to understanding the needs and agreeing on solutions.

Usually most people go along with this. It makes sense. However some people continue to resist the questioning process. To overcome this you can re-explain the necessity to confine your discussion to their needs. "I know you want to leave here today with a clear understanding of how our service relates to your company rather than talk in generalities."

We showed one prospective client a list of services early in our meeting and he revealed that he wasn't interested in training for his people but preferred a motivational speaker for his conference. It would have been a shame for us to explain our training assistance service rather than conference speaking services if we hadn't known about his needs.

You may fear that you run the chance of losing prospects by continuing to seek information about their needs. *But remember that if you don't explain key features and benefits to the prospects in a way that relates to their needs, you'll lose the sale.* So make a commitment to help customers recognize their needs. The way is simple. Ask.

Remember to make buying easy:

Become proficient at asking questions. When prospects answer, they are identifying and reinforcing their buying motive.

ACTION SHEET
Chapter 6

Ideas for Development:

1. Get the customer to express their needs immediately.
2. Play a facilitator role by asking probing questions.
3. Take the mental attitude of helping them reach their goals the best way possible.
4. Bring them back on course to help them clarify their specific needs.
5. Relate the benefits that meet their needs.
6. List other points here:
7.
8.

Of the above ideas, which one is likely to yield the best results?

What percentage of sales (or performance) increase could realistically be expected?

How long would it take: to develop the idea? to get results?

Who would have to be involved?

What date should we start?

What is the first step I should take?

Chapter 7

Don't Sell, Let Them Buy

When I first started my company, one of our management trainees did a comparative study of computers and software. We reviewed the literature and invited the best company to do a demonstration for us. I had approved the expenditure and the sale was theirs, pending the success of the demonstration.

The day came, and two people arrived to do the demonstration. They didn't ask us what we hoped to use the computer for. They just launched into their standard demonstration. We were terribly busy that day and wanted to see only one feature: the one that would merge addresses with letters. We knew the software could handle this based on its literature and previous discussions with the company.

We asked them about this feature but neither of them could demonstrate it, nor did they act the least bit interested in our questions. They continued with the standard demonstration.

IDENTIFY THE BENEFITS THAT ARE
MOST IMPORTANT TO EACH CUSTOMER

Why did neither of them seem to care about our needs? Why didn't they reassure us that the software had that capability, or offer to find out how it worked and come back? Were they afraid to admit they didn't know? Did they really think they could ignore our needs and sell their package by demonstrating features which didn't relate to our needs? Or did they perhaps not understand the importance of our question to the selling process? Whatever it was, they lost the sale.

When leaving, the two salespeople made no apology or attempt to address our need. They asked some standard closing questions that didn't relate to us. Little did they know that 25 minutes earlier when they walked in the door, the sale was practically in their hand!

Nothing stood in the way except their ability to hear our need and respond to it. Is it possible that they hadn't heard our questions about merging letters with addresses? Perhaps their minds were so intent on going through a standard list of features that they didn't recognize the importance of our questions. Or maybe they felt it was their duty to explain all the standard features even though we were only interested in one--the one they couldn't explain.

The next day we saw a different computer and software package that suited us and we bought it. The day earlier we knew nothing of this computer and would have bought the first one had they shown us the features we wanted, not the features they wanted to show.

STICK TO THEIR NEEDS

When your people are selling, are they wasting their time? Are they doing point by point demonstrations that follow a standard procedure, forgetting about what the customer needs?

Are they fooling themselves when not making a sale by blaming the product, the price, the customer or the company? Oscar Wilde, the playwright and wit, put it amusingly. Upon arriving at his English club after seeing one of his plays that had failed to please the audience, he was asked by a friend, "How was it?" Wilde replied, "The play was a great success, but the audience was a failure." Do we kid ourselves into thinking our failure is not our own?

In order to profit, every salesperson must find out what customers want and concentrate only on those needs. We only have 17 minutes in which to hold people's attention in face-to-face meetings.

Do we want to waste those 17 minutes or should we use that valuable time to discuss their needs? Shouldn't we find out which benefits interest them? To be successful we must stick to their needs, and nothing else.

JUST ASK

How do we find out what customers' needs are? The best way is to ask them! This is true of many things in life, not just sales. I remember hearing about a psychologist who had cured many people suffering from schizophrenia. These were people whom experts had deemed completely incurable.

Her patients, after their cure, moved on to become valuable members of society, as lawyers, academics--highly educated and successful people. What was the incredible secret of her success? Among the complexities of her system was one basic premise. She asked them what they needed!

Had they been mistreated when they were three or six years old? What had they missed in life? Love, attention, encouragement? She asked them what they needed and they told her. Their answers revolutionized the results that were achieved.

Have your people thought of asking their customers what they need? Perhaps if they ask more often, and concentrate only on those needs, they will revolutionize their results!

The principle of asking is simple, it's basic, and it's critical to success in anything we do. How often do we really ask people what they need?

LISTEN!

Do we know what our husbands or our wives want from marriage, or do we presume we know? Do we presume it's the same as we want or our parents wanted? Perhaps if we ask, we'll be surprised.

Perhaps we're like the computer salespeople, so busy presuming we know what the other person wants that we don't hear the needs even when they stare us right in the face.

If it's true in personal life, surely it's true in business. If we're going to discover people's needs, we have to look and listen. We have to stop presuming we know.

RECONFIRM THAT THE BENEFITS ARE RIGHT

Finally, when we do find out what the needs are, we have to prove we can meet those needs. We concentrate on the benefits that meet those needs until the benefits are crystal clear to the customer.

We have to confirm and reconfirm that the benefits are right. When we do that, the customer doesn't need to be sold to. When the benefits are right, and crystal clear, when the benefits match their needs, they buy.

Knowing the features and benefits of your product is the first step in successful selling.

The second step is deciding which features and benefits the customer wants to hear about in order to make a buying decision. This identifies the buying motive.

The chart below illustrates that a full range of benefits is possible for any product/service. It is essential when selling or promoting an idea to emphasize those benefits which are of the most interest or importance to the listener.

Identifying the Benefits That are *Most Important to Each Customer*

B	B	B	B	B	B	B	B	B
1	2	3	4	5	6	7	8	9
		X			X	X		

B = Benefits of your product/service

X = Those benefits you have decided to emphasize and explain after asking probing questions to determine the needs.

- Remember that the human attention span is limited. Some research shows that we only have 17 minutes in face-to-face presentations and as little as 2 minutes on the telephone to make an impact. Therefore we must probe effectively to find out which benefit the customer wants.

- Don't wait for the customers to tell you which benefit(s) they want; ask them!

- By asking them, you won't run the risk of jumping to conclusions and your presentation will be in line with their needs.

- By asking them what is important, you will reinforce their own thinking about their needs, make their decision process clearer and quicker, and help them to prioritize their needs.

By presenting to their needs you will save time as well as increase sales. I remember an accounting group that asked me to train 40 of their accountancy partners from around the nation. Two of the partners came to me at the beginning and said, "Mrs. Harvey, our problem in our office is too much business. In fact we're two months behind now on delivering to the clients we already have."

"Hmm," I said wondering why they were selected for the training. "Well, perhaps you could sit in and see if any of the principles can help you."

The next morning the two came rushing into the training room, smiles on their faces, waving a check. "What's happening?" I asked.

"Well we listened to your principle of asking for needs instead of doing a standard rundown of all services," they said. Then they explained that they had a breakfast meeting with a prospective client and tried the system.

"We asked the client what she needed. When she said 'trusts', we explained our expertise in trusts only. That took 20 minutes rather than the standard two hour presentation. Then we asked her if she would like to get started and she said yes, and wrote us a deposit check." Normally they said they sent out confirmation letters that created longer lead time and lost many clients!

We calculate a 20% time saving on generating clients by asking for needs," they said happily.

Think about your business. Can you shorten your response time by focusing on needs? If so you'll increase your business dramatically.

Remember to make buying easy:

Don't sell. Clear the path so they can buy.

ACTION SHEET
Chapter 7

Ideas for Development:

1. Avoid point by point customer presentation, instead
2. Remember you have 17 minutes to hold attention, make them count.
3. Probe for needs, then present points which meet those particular needs.
4. Listen and don't make presumptions.
5. Confirm and reconfirm that the benefits meet the customer needs.
6. List other points here:
7.
8.

Of the above ideas, which one is likely to yield the best results?

What percentage of sales (or performance) increase could realistically be expected?

How long would it take: to develop the idea? to get results?

Who would have to be involved?

What date should we start?

What is the first step I should take?

PART 4

HOW TO BREAK THE OBJECTION BARRIER

Chapter 8

If You Do This, You'll Never Worry About Objections

A sales objection is like smoke; if it's not cleared, it lingers. Why are objections often a nightmare to the sales force? The answer is simple.

ADOPT A POSITIVE ATTITUDE

Most people dread objections rather than welcoming them. So to deal effectively with objections, the first step is to change our attitude.

In order to do that, think about this. Would anyone buy a product without having some questions and concerns about it? Let's put ourselves in the place of the prospect and remember the last time we bought something. The decision cycle works through a questioning process. We all take in new facts, process them, ask questions or wonder silently, listen and look, and then, piece by piece, come to a decision.

Therefore, the objection process is a normal part of the buying cycle. If prospects have no questions or objections, they probably have no interest. Since that's the case, why not welcome objections? In fact, theoretically, the more questions and objections, the more interest there is. No one asks questions when they're not interested.

Why not think of objections as an integral part of the whole sales process? It's something to work with from beginning to end. The fact is that the whole sales process is an objection encountering process.

If we become comfortable with this fact, then we can develop the most effective methods of dealing with it.

HIT OBJECTIONS HEAD ON

Ignoring objections can be fatal! No one likes to be ignored. We can't try to ignore objections. If we ignore the prospects' concern, we are discounting their needs. We must hear the concern and acknowledge it in such a way that the prospect knows we've heard it.

Would we continue to see a doctor if every time we mentioned a problem, he ignored it and kept talking about something else? Of course not.

The same is true in selling. *The biggest mistake is trying to sweep objections under the rug.* We must listen and recognize the objection, then work with the customers to clarify the issue if we are to build their commitment.

BE THE FIRST TO BRING UP THE OBJECTION

Do you find in your businesses that certain objections are brought out repeatedly in each selling situation? For most companies this is true. They each have objections peculiar to their business. Salespeople get better results if they hit objections head on. You can actually bring up the subject before the prospects do!

This is an excellent system because it puts the prospect's mind at ease. It's comforting to know that the objection has been dealt with and overcome before with other customers. By bringing up the objection first, and proving you've dealt with it, you let the prospect know that you are truly interested in the welfare of your customers. That builds trust and trust builds a relationship that succeeds.

Recognize Three Forms of Objections

To become adept at working with objections we need to be able to recognize them.

Objections take three forms: questions; statements; and last, but not least, non-verbal actions of uneasiness or uncertainty. Here are three examples.

Questions

Let's say a prospect is taking a tour of your factory. When talking about how your products are stocked, the prospect asks, "How much of your work is off-the-shelf and how much is built to specification?"

Statements

Or she makes a statement, "Most of our suppliers deliver within seven days of our order. I presume you do this too."

Non-Verbal Actions

Or she says nothing, but when passing through your factory with you, pauses at one particular production stage. You wonder why. Perhaps she has a negative impression that is wrong. If you ask, you can clear up the doubt immediately. If you let it go, the bad impression will stick and it will linger forever like smoke.

ASK "WHY DO YOU ASK?"

Regardless of how the objection is brought to your attention, you need to probe to get to the bottom of the matter. In the three examples above, what are the prospects really asking? All three may be asking themselves if you can meet their delivery requirements.

In the first question about off-the-shelf versus specification work, they may fear that you spend so much time on specials that you won't have stock built up when they need it. You need to find out the reasons for questions: "Why do you ask?"

If they have the wrong impression, you can correct it. If they have the right impression, you can reinforce it. "Oh, yes, we always have stock on hand."

In the next example, the customer makes a statement about their customary seven-day delivery from suppliers. They are probably looking for an acknowledgment from you that you can match or better this.

Here's your chance to push a benefit and make it come alive with a story. If you can deliver in three days, you'll want to let them know and give them an example for reassurance.

"Yes, in fact we pride ourselves on our prompt delivery capability. Just recently, Jim Smith, our client across town, called our production director to thank him for getting him out of a tight spot. His supplies ran low and we got him a delivery within the day. This kept his production line going, and of course he appreciates our efforts."

Then tell them what you'll do for them. "Our normal practice is three-day delivery." Then you'll want to follow up with a confirming question: "Would that be important to you in working with us?"

UNCOVER THE REAL DOUBT OR FEAR

In the third example, the prospect pauses at one production point without commenting. You, of course, sense the prospect's uneasiness and probe to see what's on their mind. You might say, "Is that similar to other processes you've seen?" or another question to open the conversation. Your purpose is to uncover the real doubt or fear.

If you discover they're worried about a bottleneck in production possibly leading to late deliveries, you can put their minds at ease and turn the subject into a benefit by citing a good example.

It will answer any doubts, and it will clear up the objection so that it doesn't linger.

To improve your sales effectiveness, find out the reasons for people asking questions and making statements. Watch their behavior. When you pick up nonverbal messages you'll be amazed what you discover. What you learn can change your business, and your life.

Here's an experiment you can do.

Focus your energy for a two-hour period each day on really looking, listening, and asking. Do it at work and at home. You'll be amazed at the increase in communication, at the increased understanding of people and their needs, and most importantly at your own satisfaction from these dealings.

Too often we presume we know what people are thinking. When we really look, listen, and ask, we find out differently. People communicate their feelings and objections in many ways. The way they act is as important as the words they use. Don't miss it.

And don't forget to ask questions. In their best selling book on principled negotiation, *Getting to Yes*, Roger Fisher and William Urytalk about the importance of finding out people's interests and reasons before negotiating. That way, the results can meet everyone's needs. Fisher and Ury believe everyone should benefit. If this method of asking questions is beneficial to high-power negotiations, then it can be beneficial to us in our sales development.

Remember to Break the Objection Barrier:

Never worry about objections: hit them head on.

ACTION SHEET
Chapter 8

Ideas for Development:

1. Remember that an objection is like smoke. It lingers if it's not cleared.
2. Welcome objections as part of the sales process.
3. Be the first to bring up an objection which is standard.
4. Recognize the three forms of objections: questions, statements and non-verbal actions.
5. Ask, "Why do you ask?" to uncover objections or misunderstandings.
6. List other points here:
7.
8.

Of the above ideas, which one is likely to yield the best results?

What percentage of sales (or performance) increase could realistically be expected?

How long would it take: to develop the idea? to get results?

Who would have to be involved?

What date should we start?

What is the first step I should take?

Chapter 9

A 3-Step Formula for Turning Objections into Approvals

There's one critical thing that many people in sales overlook. That's the fact that *buyers must feel we hear and understand their objection.* This is imperative. If they don't, all the logical arguments in the world won't convince them. We must prove we hear. This we call 'cushioning the objection,' or *empathy.*

Here's a very effective three-step formula for turning objections into approvals. It's simple, easy, and, if carried out properly, gets tremendous results. When a customer has an objection, do this:

1. The Cushioning/Empathetic Segment
2. The Explanatory Segment
3. The Close-Off or Recycle Segment

The amount of time we give each segment depends on the complexity and severity of the objection. A mild objection could be handled by combining all three segments in just a sentence or two. A severe objection could require a long period of time for each segment. The important thing is to go through all three steps on each and every objection.

Let's look at some actual examples. In our training and motivational speaking business prospective clients sometimes wonder how we can help them without having technical knowledge of their product. They might say, "I like the practical approach of your service, but I wonder how you can help without knowing about the technical aspects of our business."

SHOW, TALK AND PROVE YOUR CONCERN

The first step is the cushion. Show understanding. "Yes, John, I can certainly understand your concern."

Don't stop there; this is a serious objection, fundamental to the whole discussion. "In fact, this is the same concern that most other clients have the first time they come to see us." Here you're showing John that you not only understand, you're even open enough to agree that others have the same concern.

You're now starting to be reliable in his eyes. At the same time, you're giving him a positive indication that the problem can be solved by using the term 'most other clients.' You wouldn't have clients if the problem couldn't be solved.

You continue, "I know that you must have this point absolutely clarified or you won't be confident about our service."

Now you're further agreeing with his concern and starting to link his concern with an explanation by saying he must have the point clarified. This puts him in a receptive frame of mind to receive the explanation, providing you've done enough cushioning to suit his personality and the severity of the objection. If you don't do this step, you're lost. Why? Because, without a cushion, the explanations bounce back as if they were arrows hitting a brick wall. An explanation will never penetrate the buyer's mind if the objection isn't cleared first.

There's a straightforward reason for this. Part of the buyer's mind is still distracted by doubt. The doubt causes a mental shield to go up. Most of your explanation can't penetrate the shield because the buyer's mind is taken up with the objection.

You have to *prove* you hear and understand the objection, or your explanation falls on deaf ears. When you do prove to the buyer that you understand, the shield starts to disintegrate, allowing your explanations to penetrate. Eventually, the shield breaks down completely if your cushion and explanation are sufficient. If they're not sufficient, you have to start all over again. You cushion again and explain again.

EXPLAIN THE REASONS

When you've done enough cushioning, you move on to the explanation: "I mentioned earlier that we combine our training and motivational expertise with your company's technical expertise. Of course, in order to do this we need to understand all the key factors that influence our client's sales. These include the product benefits, the management policies, the competition, and so on. Otherwise we couldn't do our job."

This has two components. In the first part you're starting the explanation. In the last sentence you're cushioning again, agreeing that his concern is valid. If you didn't understand his company, you couldn't do the job.

Now you want to continue the explanation, and start to let John see the benefits of working with you. This will move you closer to getting his approval.

"Most of our clients have been running their own companies many years. We can't learn everything they know, but we need to learn as much as possible in a short time. So, when we start working with clients we do an intensive briefing session."

Now, still in the explanation stage, you want to confirm that the message is getting through and start to build consensus. This is a good time for a question or two.

"Can you see how that works?" Then you might want to produce some evidence. Remember that a picture is worth a thousand words and will stay in the memory longer. He will forget 80% of what you tell him within two days.

"If we work together, we'll talk with you in depth. Some clients tell us that the questions we ask, plus the analysis we do, gives them new food for thought. Often they say that the questions we ask and the analysis we do is useful to them in increasing sales." Now you're giving him a mental picture of how it works, and the extra benefits he can get.

"John, would you like to see one of our briefing questionnaires? We usually fax or email it to clients a week before the briefing so that they can prepare for it ahead. Would it help you to look at it?" If he says no, he's probably satisfied. If yes, he's either still skeptical or really interested. Continue until you find out.

Ask If the Concern is Satisfied

That's the reason for the next step. We must clarify whether the prospect is satisfied or not satisfied, by moving into the close-off or recycle segment. "Does that satisfy your concern about how we work with clients effectively without previously knowing about their business?"

If you get an emphatic yes and you're satisfied that he is sure, you can consider it closed.

If you get a 'yes, but,' you recycle all three steps, the cushion, the explanation, and the close-off. Start with the cushion, again. You probe more deeply into his concern again, just as you did at first, so that you can provide a more appropriate cushion statement.

Since he's not satisfied, you know that either your cushion or your explanation was not satisfactory to him. So start with the cushion.

If you go straight to more explanation as most people tend to do, you'll run the risk of losing the sale. Going back to the cushion never hurts and always helps.

Even if your problem is in the factual part of the explanation, going back to the cushion will satisfy his human need to be heard and valued for his concerns. After you cushion his concern--proving beyond a shadow of a doubt that you understand his objection and reason for the objection-- then you can go on to the explanation.

In the explanation segment, you tell him the features and the benefits. Perhaps you can't overcome his objection, but you can offer alternatives. Perhaps the alternatives will make up a better package than he expected and overcome the objection. You might be able to supply eight out of 10 of his requirements whereas the competitor can only offer seven out of 10, so never give up.

Then you move again into the close-off segment. "Does that answer your question?" or, "Does that satisfy your concern?"

When people object, there's always a reason. Find out why. Be concerned. Then you're free to move onto the explanation, the benefits, and the order!

Remember to Break the Objection Barrier:

Start by proving you understand the objection.

ACTION SHEET
Chapter 9

Ideas for Development:

1. Use the cushioning segment to prove that you understand the objection before explaining the answer.
2. Follow the cushion with the explanation.
3. Give your customer a mental picture of how your service works.
4. Ask if the concern is satisfied after the explanation.
5. If the customer still has concerns, start the 3-part process again.
6. List other points here:
7.
8.

Of the above ideas, which one is likely to yield the best results?

What percentage of sales (or performance) increase could realistically be expected?

How long would it take: to develop the idea? to get results?

Who would have to be involved?

What date should we start?

What is the first step I should take?

PART 5

SIX WAYS TO STOP LOSING BUSINESS NEEDLESSLY

Chapter 10

Why is 75% of All Business Lost ... on a Customer's First Contact with a Company?

Yes, it's true: statistics prove that 75% of all business is lost on a customer's first contact with companies. Who is responsible for this?

WHO IS RESPONSIBLE?

The answer is straightforward. It's *anyone* ever having, at *any time, any* contact with *any customer* or *any buyer.*

One of our clients, Ian, said, "I like to make everybody in my company think of themselves as involved in a sales organization."

"The time has gone," says Ian, "when any manufacturer like ourselves can afford to think of themselves as only manufacturing."

Ian has an important point. Everyone in a company should realize that without customers there is no business. But how many people do? If they did, would 75% of our potential business be lost?

Who's responsible? We've already said everyone's responsible who has contact with our customers and buyers. Does this include the receptionist, the service department, people in production, finance, and so on?

In our sales and sales management seminars, we work with the attendees to determine which employees, in which departments, influence sales. In this chapter we're going to take you through the same steps. When people realize how much potential business is lost by non-sales personnel, some real changes start taking place in organizations. They learn ways to develop harmony between departments and ways to motivate everyone to think of the customer as an integral part of their jobs. People start to realize that their livelihood depends on gaining and keeping customers.

If we're going to find out exactly where 75% of business is lost in our own companies, we have to look under every stone. We have to be open-minded and look at our companies through new eyes--the eyes of the buyers.

BEWARE: CONTACT POINTS ARE CRITICAL

We have to look at every department, our practices and our people. Of all the "contact points"--those having customer and buyer contact--we'll probably find that the 80/20 rule applies.

That narrows down our task. No doubt the 20% of our people having customer contact will have 80% of the influence. We can start there.

Who are they? Every company has a first contact point. That's a good place to start. Is it the switchboard operator or the receptionist perhaps?

Gordon Watson told me about a talk he gave once at a retailers' meeting. He asked the group, "Who do you think is the most important person in your company? Is it the president?"

Then he went on and asked the group to visualize a pyramid. At the top of the pyramid sat the head of the company. Yes, he or she was important.

Under him, in the next level of the pyramid, sat the directors, the next level the senior managers, then more levels of managers, then the supervisors.

Then, all the layers forming the foundation of the pyramid were the members of staff. At the very cornerstone of the pyramid sat the receptionist or the switchboard operator.

That person and that person alone was the customer's contact.

The customer doesn't know the people at the top of the pyramid. To them all that matters is their contact point-- that's the most important person.

REALIZE THE IMPORTANCE OF EACH CONTACT POINT

How many companies regard their switchboard operator as their most important person?

Ian and I were discussing his philosophy of training his people to respond as a sales organization. He said he noticed that other companies sometimes bring in temporary help. The first place they seem to put the 'temp' is on reception or the switchboard.

How can new people on their first day on the job carry out the most important function in the company?

Try as they might, they can't possibly know all the people in the company in order to handle incoming calls effectively. They can't possibly know the products or the customers.

TRAIN AND MOTIVATE THEM TO WIN BUSINESS, NOT LOSE IT

If we want to stop losing business, we have to concentrate on contact points. Which are yours? When you identify them, you can start to take action to train and motivate them to win business and not lose it.

To dramatically increase business, make a list of possible ways business is lost in your company. Then be persistent and inventive about changing them.

Dave Goillon was determined to take action. Dave owned a company that manufactured equipment for the broadcast industry. He became conscious of the importance of the customer's first impression and decided to take some quick and effective action.

What should be done, he wondered? Previously he had success with training videos and so he found one that focused on answering the telephone. Showing it brought excellent results. First, he made it available only to the receptionist and secretaries.

TRY THREE RINGS

They caught onto the idea that customers shouldn't be made to wait long periods while phones ring. They made up a sign for reception that said 'Three Rings.' Soon everyone was asking what the sign meant. They liked the idea and decided it was good sense not to keep customers waiting, even between departments when their call is transferred.

After that, if you walked into the manufacturing facility, you would see people in every department--not just sales, but also service, testing, and so on, answering their phone before the third ring. Do you think this kind of responsiveness leads to more business? Dave and his people are sure it does. The 'Three Rings' motto keeps the importance of the customer in the forefront of everyone's minds.

It shows what can be done with a little time and forethought to the problem. Dave took action to get his people trained and motivated. He got results.

TAKE RESPONSIBILITY FOR EMPLOYEE PERFORMANCE

A few years ago, during one of our recessionary times, I wrote a letter to the editor of a major paper.

In it I said, "Isn't it up to management to take responsibility for the attitude and skill of their people?"

Some managers contend that employees have no concept of how their job relates to customers, to the business of the company, and to the economy in general, and can't be taught.

I disagree. In my letter, I said, "Isn't it time we take our head out of the sand and bring people into line with economic reality?" Bad business practices bring less business and less business brings fewer jobs. If we want our corporate world to prosper, let's stop making excuses for people's performance and start taking responsibility.

From the response that flowed in after the editorial letter was printed, I know others agree with me. Now is the time for action.

Jim Kearns, who has run both American and British companies, believes: "Words don't mean anything, unless we do something."

Let's all be sure we do something to identify the places where business is being lost and take steps to correct it. Let's not take the attitude that some managers have taken, that people can't be enlightened.

ATTITUDES – SOME NEED TO BE CHANGED

I remember one day sitting in a university classroom when the business class professor told us a story. "See that row of 20 apartment buildings across the street? There are 12 apartments in each building."

"The owner of those buildings hasn't paid income tax for the last nine years! Not a penny!" Gasps came from everyone. "Imagine, a rich person like that not paying income tax." It confirmed the suspicions of most of us in the room who had no experience of wealth creation at that stage of our lives. We thought, "Yes, wealth creators are indeed villains, leaving the rest of us to pay taxes who could ill afford it by comparison."

Next the professor said, "I know that man. He started with only $100 years ago when he bought his first apartment. He borrowed the down payment from family and friends. Then he worked at two jobs--one during the day, the other at night to pay off his debt. On weekends he worked to paint and repair the buildings. The first few years were really blood, sweat, and tears. Gradually he made enough money to buy another building and another."

"Due to his hard work and his willingness to risk his capital, he has provided housing and jobs for hundreds of people. Because of his policy of keeping his property in top notch condition, there were jobs created for painters, plumbers, gardeners, and electricians. His apartments are also creating a demand for supplies: carpets, curtains, kitchen appliances, and so on, which are creating other businesses and more jobs. Where would we be without people who were willing to take these risks to keep money and jobs in circulation? In addition, he pays taxes on all products and services he buys."

There you have it. I suddenly had a new perspective on wealth creation. It changed my thinking from that point on. The change came from the vivid step-by-step understanding of the process of job creation and money circulation.

We know that perspectives can be changed. People usually just need someone to enlighten them. Otherwise they carry around preconceived ideas that go unexamined until someone gives them new facts that change the way they look at things. But the enlightenment has to come in a way that they personally find logical, not as take-it-or-leave-it facts. We all know that from our own past experience.

If the professor hadn't used the step-by-step process and instead said, "People with money create jobs, you should support them," what do you think our level of acceptance would be? You're right; zero--because we wouldn't have built up our own mental picture of the links in the chain of the process. Instead we'd have held to our old picture--the preconceived idea that didn't link wealth and job creation together.

MAKE PEOPLE REALIZE THAT THE CUSTOMER PAYS THEIR SALARIES

The point is that employees who don't link their own job to the value of the customer haven't been enlightened. And they are not going to change their idea because some manager comes in and says to them, You must stop coming in five minutes late in the morning. Think of all the customer calls you're missing." It doesn't make a link with them.

They have to be made to understand that without customers, there is no company, and without a company, there are no jobs--not even their own.

If you can turn someone from a non-capitalist to a capitalist with one easy story, think what results you can get when you make employees understand the value of the customer.

Someone has to take the time to sit down and explain to them, that without customer there will be no jobs, including their own. Otherwise, people continue with preconceived ideas. It's our responsibility as managers to make sure they understand the value of the customer and handle their job effectively.

When Gordon Watson was addressing the Retailer's Association about the importance of the customer's first contact, what do you think he had in mind about the way people should be treated?

WHAT'S THE COMMON THREAD?

Let's take the most successful companies. What do the heads of those companies, sitting at the top of the pyramid, believe about the ways customers should be treated? What's the common thread that makes them successful?

Think of the companies you most like dealing with and you'll know the answer. Chances are that your requests are treated with care and concern. Besides offering a good product, the companies pay attention to human needs. They treat you with the courtesy and respect that good customers deserve.

If, on the other hand, you deal with a company whose employees take an offhand approach to you and your needs, you'll probably go somewhere else.

When I think of exceptional service, I think of my first printer, Chris Marson. I remember meeting him on a Sunday many years ago to review some proofs. Although his back was out, he kept his date and came to the appointment with a painful limp. His service has always been impeccable. Even though his printing presses are running seven days a week and Chris never has a spare moment, he always makes time to come to the phone with a friendly, "Hello, Christine, how are you, alright? Good to hear from you," and his voice says he means it. He knows that price and service are essential but not everything. He knows the value of the human factor.

THINK OF WAYS TO TREAT PROSPECTS
WITH A PERSONAL TOUCH

What areas of your business require attention to 'the human factor' in dealing with your customers? If you concentrate your thoughts on this, you'll develop ideas which relate to your buyers. You'll retain some of that 75% of potential business that slips away.

Here's an example of what we did when I first started my company. We analyzed our operation and decided that not enough personal attention was being given to prospective clients at their first visit to us. Since we were in a communal office building at the time, we had no control over the reception area. Sometimes visitors were greeted professionally and sometimes not, depending on who was on duty. We knew that the first few minutes the prospects waited were critical to their judgment of us.

We had to take drastic action. We put together a two-part plan that at the time seemed a little 'over the top.' But we had to try something.

Here's what we did to overcome the questionable reception. First we called visitors several days before the meeting to confirm the appointment and we did one more thing to give it a personal touch. "Mr. Jones, we're looking forward to seeing you on Tuesday at 3:00. By the way, we like to have everyone's coffee ready when they arrive. How do you like yours?"

The results were very good. We had previously worried that people would think this was silly, but they didn't. They liked the personal touch. They even commented on how nice it was to work with people who took the time and trouble over personal details.

The second part of our new policy was to go out into the reception area *immediately* upon their arrival. If the conference room wasn't ready, we chatted with them for a few minutes in reception while it was being prepared. Again, the results were remarkable. People liked being personally attended to. They also had no time to focus on the reception.

It proved to pay off handsomely--our conversion of prospects to clients went up immediately. Furthermore, the new clients started to openly talk to us about the procedures.

They told us how impressed they were with the way we handled our business. They thought it was marketing at its best. Ian McCallum was one of the people who visited us during that time. He said he liked everything from the sales presentation to the smallest personal detail--even our attention to how people like their coffee. It taught us a lesson. We now know how important the human factor is. We also know that sometimes you have to be inventive to solve human factor problems.

The human factor is important in every business. Some people use it instinctively, and therefore are tremendously successful in business. Others don't, and they lose business needlessly despite having superior products or services. Watch the way you're treated the next time you buy something. It will give you a wealth of ideas on how to and how not to treat customers. *Then decide for yourself what changes to make.*

All companies have areas in which the human factor can be improved. What areas are these in your company? If you identify these and give them creative solutions, you'll prevent business from being lost needlessly. If you're thinking about new ways to generate business, think about this one. When you stop losing business, you are, in effect, creating a new way to generate business.

Remember to stop losing business needlessly:

Regain the lost 75% of sales—make everyone responsible for treating prospects and customers like gold.

ACTION SHEET
Chapter 10

Ideas for Development:

1. Make a list of all non-sales personnel who have contact with prospects by telephone or in person. Include switchboard operators, delivery and service personnel.
2. Train and motivate them to win business, not lose it.
3. Try the three rings system.
4. Make people realize that the customer pays their salary.
5. Think of ways to treat prospects with a personal touch.
6. Make everyone responsible for treating prospects and customers like gold.
7. List other points here:
8.

Of the above ideas, which one is likely to yield the best results?

What percentage of sales (or performance) increase could realistically be expected?

How long would it take: to develop the idea? to get results?

Who would have to be involved?

What date should we start?

What is the first step I should take?

Chapter 11

Successful Interface Among Finance, Production, Sales, and Service: Is It Essential?

A trade delegation from abroad not long ago visited a factory in the Washington D.C. area. They had a budget of $25 million. They wanted to visit companies and were ready to sign contracts for equipment they needed.

The US Government Liaison Official called one factory to arrange a visit for the next day. He informed them that the delegation wanted to see machinery demonstrations.

NO ONE THERE TO FINALIZE SALES?

The next day the delegation duly arrived. They were greeted by the production director and given a demonstration. There was no one from the sales department on hand to assist. The delegates were impressed and several were ready to place their orders. But, would you believe, they were told by the production director that there was no one to finalize sales details! So they moved on to a competitor's factory and placed their order there!

'What happened to the internal communication of the first factory?" Bill and I asked in amazement as we talked with the government official who related the story to us. "Well, the production department heard that the delegation wanted a demonstration tour and nobody at the company thought they were coming to buy!" he said. As a result they lost that important sale..

This true story exemplifies how easy it is for people, including key employees and even directors, to lose sight of the fact that they are in business to sell.

The three vital questions to ask ourselves are:

1. Are all our people trained to recognize a sales inquiry?

2. Do we have a way of alerting sales teams of sudden important inquiries so that sales can take place?

3. Do other directors in the company have the authority to finalize sales when necessary?

If this had been the case with the above company they would be much richer today. Maintaining sales through a good interface between departments is essential. What steps can you take to improve the link?

Very often in our seminars on developing effective sales we have a wide range of staff members, not just salespeople. Some come from production, some from finance, and so on. They learn, alongside sales managers and sales staff, how other departments can win and lose business. The results are enlightening.

OVERCOME RESISTANCE TO SELLING

It's not easy to make everyone in the company feel they are in business to sell. Yet, as we discussed in the last chapter, the more progressive companies are doing just that--and making a success of it.

Several years ago I was lecturing to a group of bank, and the area manager who was in charge of 24 branches told me his secret of success.

"Every month I get my branch managers together and I tell them to remember that they are salespeople," he said. "With over 50 different services to offer, and customers to keep happy, they cannot afford to think of themselves as anything else."

EVERYONE LIVES BY SELLING SOMETHING!

Robert Louis Stevenson said in the late 1800s, "Everyone lives by selling something." Managers can create attitude changes so that effective training can take place. It's not an easy job, but who said success comes easily?

Will you run into resistance from employees who don't believe their job relates to sales? Dave Goillon found resistance from his engineers when it came to sales training. Even though technical inquiries came directly to them, they didn't feel that sales related to them. Dave tried to entice them by offering a training film designed for non-sales personnel, but they weren't convinced they needed it.

BE CREATIVE IN TRAINING NON-SALES PERSONNEL TO BE SALES SAVVY

Dave considered his options. "I could have forced it on them, but I knew I needed their cooperation. Since the video unit was in their area, I decided to show it to another group and let the engineers just observe." It wasn't long before the engineers were requesting a showing of their own. Dave used the principle that there's nothing worse than feeling left out of training.

If others are learning something useful, everyone wants their share. By creating eagerness, he got results when a direct approach failed. He achieved the training that was needed.

The engineers then kept a message pad by the phone to record every prospect's name, phone number, and inquiry. Dave estimated that a substantial increase in sales occurred because of improved customer service, and the improved tracking system. Awareness and training paid off.

IMPROVE RELATIONSHIPS BETWEEN DEPARTMENTS

Large companies face the same problems with relationships between sales and other departments.

I once sponsored a scholarship program called the *Most Promising Young Businesswoman Award*. Part of the award was a sales internship that we arranged with a leading FORTUNE 500 company. This company had a fine reputation for high quality office equipment. They had a superb sales training program, recognized internationally.

The award winner spent three weeks with them, first having theoretical sales training and then time with salespeople on the road. As a follow-up, she spent a week in an after-sales department, where delivery schedules were implemented. "Much to my amazement," she said, "I discovered that the service department had no idea how difficult sales were to achieve. In fact, they often treated new sales indifferently. They paid little attention to delivery schedules and didn't realize how easily they could lose sales!"

STYMIED BY INDIFFERENCE

They spent little time in communicating with the sales department if there were outstanding questions relating to the paperwork. They failed to recognize that a sale could be jeopardized by delay or indifference. The whole sales effort seemed stymied by their indifference.

After graduation from university, she interviewed for many high-power jobs. The interviewers were intrigued with her sales internship and asked what important lessons she learned. Her answer: "The importance of good liaison between sales and other departments. To have a good sales department is not enough." Her insight landed her a prestigious position in international banking, marketing its services to aerospace industries. Later she was transferred to Singapore and held one of the top positions in Asia with her organization. Her lesson served her well.

AWARENESS BRINGS UNDERSTANDING

Jim Kearns has proved the value of getting internal support to ensure sales collaboration from all departments. He believes that awareness brings understanding, and that understanding brings cooperation. He's developed a unique and effective way of bringing it about.

ACHIEVE A 100 FOLD INCREASE

While heading up the international division of his company, Jim took sales of their products in the US from $150,000 to $15,000,000 in a seven-year period.

To build a solid base for his expansion, Jim knew he had to build everyone's awareness of sales in order to get their cooperation. Only with this cooperation between departments could he continue to dramatically increase sales.

Here's what Jim told me. "On the last Friday of every month I run a sales meeting for my department. At that meeting we have what we call 'Highlights and Lowlights.' Everyone informally tells about the highlights--the goals that were met, and the lowlights--the goals that still need attention."

There are no notes other than the secretary's and no formal paperwork. "Everyone is relaxed and the atmosphere is supportive." Jim is careful to bring up sensitive subjects such as incomplete goals in a casual, supportive way. "I want to give confidence to those involved that they can accomplish their goals." This subtlety, he finds, makes people want to use their full skills and effort to reach their goals.

CREATE A COOPERATIVE CAMPAIGN

But Jim doesn't end his cooperative campaign there with only his department! He invites other key department employees to join in after the internal proceedings have finished.

He says, "The Friday meeting starts about 4:00 and runs until about 5:30. Then we invite guests from other departments. This gives the International Division a chance to recount successes and explain the needs and expectation for the future."

The value is twofold. First, it provides vital awareness, understanding, and support from other departments. Second, it provides the equally important communication and motivation within his department. Now Jim's department gets support from other departments in a way that far surpasses formal meetings of any kind.

When I talked with Jim about his secrets of success, it seemed to me that there was a lot more planning behind these meetings than met the eye. Was it really a casual, impromptu evening where everyone spoke off the cuff? Perhaps not. Jim's people know he has high expectations of them and they see the Friday meetings as an important time to acknowledge their successes.

Does Jim run the meeting off-the-cuff, with no notes? No. He's careful to review the notes before each meeting, so that he can bring up unresolved issues or give credit where it's due.

Would your company benefit from a 100-fold increase in seven years as his company did?

ACKNOWLEDGE THE BACK OFFICE

Stuart Sanders, who was head of a financial futures company, found that he was able to improve the relationship between departments by acknowledging the value of the people behind the scenes.

"I never dismiss our back-office people, because I know they are one of our biggest assets. They are the final link in the chain. If the final link is unsupportive or uncooperative, the customer can be lost. If this happens, all the effort leading up to that point is also lost."

Stuart has found that sales training for his non-frontliners has paid big dividends. It has opened their eyes to the problems of the sales force and the value of good customer relations.

DON'T WAIT FOR OTHERS

Could you personally benefit from better interface between departments? Undoubtedly there are people in your workplace who influence your working style, your attitude, your job satisfaction. Are you waiting for them to take the first step? Are you waiting for them to improve the situation? It may never happen.

Why wait? Why not take the first step at home, on the job, in the community? Let those around you see how their activities link to your activities. Let them see the areas of mutual interest and the gain to be had from better cooperation. Your reward will be immediate satisfaction. Why not make a greater effort now and see what results you get?

What steps can you take to increase the interface between departments? Look at every possibility. Be creative. The results will speak for themselves.

Remember to stop losing business needlessly:

**Educate and motivate all departments
to support sales.**

ACTION SHEET
Chapter 11

Ideas for Development:

1. Train everyone to recognize a sales inquiry.
2. Make sure someone is trained and available to finalize sales every minute of the day, even when the sales department is away.
3. Be creative in training non-sales personnel to be sales savvy through training films, all-inclusive meetings, etc.
4. Give recognition to back office and non-sales personnel for their sales support.
5. Don't wait for others to take the first step for improving relations between departments.
6. List other points here:
7.
8.

Of the above ideas, which one is likely to yield the best results?

What percentage of sales (or performance) increase could realistically be expected?

How long would it take: to develop the idea? to get results?

Who would have to be involved?

What date should we start?

What is the first step I should take?

Chapter 12

The Lost Inquiry:
More Common Than You Think!

Does your company have an accountant? What an absurd question, you might ask. All companies have someone in charge of keeping track of the money. The bigger the company, the more people they have keeping track.

But what about sales inquiries? Who keeps track of them? One person? Several people? No one? Is there a system or a set of books to track inquiries just as we keep books to track money in and money out?

Imagine it--no company worth its salt would 'not' have a system to track their money. Yet they often don't have systems for tracking sales 'inquiries' and sales in progress.

TREAT INQUIRIES LIKE GOLD

Isn't an inquiry as good as cash? Didn't you spend money to generate the inquiry? Perhaps you advertised and publicized your product. You spent years in product development to make sure you had the very best product possible for your customer. Yet, when it comes to the sales inquiry, do you treat it like gold? No, most don't even treat it as well as they treat cash.

With cash, every penny is recorded. When one penny is missing, people want to know why. But what happens when an inquiry is missing? Usually no one notices. Probably, unlike money, there was no one responsible for tracking all the sales leads and inquiries coming in.

Perhaps the salespeople keep their own leads. If so, where do they keep them? In the safe, like money? No. More likely in the briefcase, the drawer, the filing cabinet, the car, the house, the jacket pocket. Not just one of those places, but all of those places.

Since we don't trust money like that, why should we treat leads--an equally important commodity--like that? Isn't it true that if our tracking system is less effective than our accounting system we cannot expect accuracy and reliability? It's certain that we are not getting the results we should.

CREATE THE PERFECT ACTION PROVOKING SYSTEM

There's more to tracking than meets the eye. In tracking the inquiry we should record:

1. The date the sales inquiry comes in.
2. The date the sales inquiry should be acted upon.
3. The date the sales inquiry was acted upon.
4. The date the sales inquiry should next be acted upon.
5. The date the sales inquiry turned into a sale or the sale was lost.

Then there are categories of leads. A good way to split up the leads in your mind is to think of two distinct groups of leads: the conventional and the unconventional leads.

On a flight from Boston to Tampa, I was talking to the district manager of a company that does demographic studies for fast food companies. They always use his service to project the growth in areas before opening a new restaurant. I immediately thought of a client I could refer him to.

We were discussing how he generates business and he told me they had a perfect system for keeping track of their sales inquiries. Every inquiry that is recorded is followed up diligently and on time.

Then he told me that half of their business was from referrals. "Great," I said, "How does a referred lead, like mine, enter your system?" "Oh," he said, "no prospects actually enter our system unless they call in or write." Then he paused and reflected. "Oops," he said, "now I see why you asked. Half of our potential business is not being followed up because it doesn't enter the system!" That's what I mean by unconventional leads.

WHAT PERCENTAGE OF YOUR BUSINESS COMES FROM UNCONVENTIONAL LEADS?

Every company has some standard, traditional ways of generating business interest, and these we call the traditional leads. These could be advertising responses, direct mail responses, exhibition responses, and so on.

Every company also has nontraditional, nonstandard ways it gets business. These we call the unconventional leads.

These could be leads gained as casually as meeting a prospective customer at a friend's house, a party, or while traveling. It could be referrals from others, a call-in, and so on. Much to a company's surprise, they often find that very big sales are generated through these nontraditional channels. Yet when an inquiry comes up, they don't necessarily put it into their system for follow-up. It often remains just a card in someone's pocket.

DEVELOP AN AIRTIGHT TRACKING SYSTEM

The point is that both categories can suffer from ineffective follow-up if an airtight system is not developed.

If you already have a system, the question is, how airtight is it? Who is responsible for receiving the inquiry, for logging it, for acting on it initially, for following it up later? Who's responsible for monitoring all inquiries at each of the above stages? Where are the records kept for ease of management review?

How are the records kept? A tracking system which is both *easy to use* and *easy to monitor* is essential. It takes time and effort to develop. It usually needs modification as the company grows or develops new services. It must be developed by someone who understands and controls the departments which will interface on the logging, action, follow-up, and so on. Otherwise, the system may not be compatible with each department.

Spot the Weaknesses

Let's look at a company that is losing business needlessly due to weak tracking and follow-up. Here's how they handle their business, step by step. Where do you see the weaknesses?

Which Ones Are Wrong?

- The company promotes its service through direct mail, sending letters, literature, and reply cards to likely users.

- It attends one exhibition per year.

- It puts advertisements in journals that have reader response cards, on a monthly basis.

- The mailing and email results in responses from interested parties almost on a daily basis.

- The sales managers distribute them to the sales force, according to territory, at the weekly sales meeting.

- The secretary logs the number of responses given to each.

- The sales force then calls each prospect to get an appointment.

- If successful, they mail or email product literature to them before the appointment.

- The salespeople keep their own records according to individual habits.

- The sales managers occasionally ask if the quality of the leads are good.

- The sales managers focus on the number of appointments each week, rather than on how the leads are being tracked or followed up.

The managers feel that good salespeople have a good system and don't need close monitoring.

What would you expect the lost business ratio to be for this company based on the management of inquiries as described above?

This company is losing a tremendous amount of its sales needlessly. Their average loss on the Harvey-Sykes scale is 60%!

If they stopped losing this business they could have a 150% increase in sales.

Let's look at this carefully because the company is spending a lot of money on what should be a sound lead-generating system, but is losing it on the follow-up.

The advertising and direct mail are sound because they are generating valid leads. But the follow-up is weak.

FIND THE CURE

What could they do to save the 60% lost business? Let's look at it from the top down. With their current system there is no uniformity in the way leads are handled. Therefore, there is no management control. When there is no management control, how can one plan growth for the future and actively control it?

The company needs a uniform tracking system that the sales manager or the head of the company can access on a regular basis. The system should record each attempt to contact the prospects, conversations held, visits, and so on.

THE MANAGEMENT CURE

If you're not in management, but you want to improve your own results, you can create your own system.

You or the managers should have *daily or weekly activity reports* showing the number of conversations actually held, the ratio of sales conversions to appointments, the number of sales plus the value of each new sale. Then they could judge consistency of effort and spot trouble areas before they become problems.

In the previous example to spot the weakness, you may have noticed that the managers' *timing* also leaves a lot to be desired. Perhaps they enjoy passing out leads at the sales meeting. But so what? It may liven up the meeting, or give the sales manager a sense of power, but it does nothing for sales efficiency.

The lead could be almost a week old before reaching the sales force. By that time it's probably stale. Then, when you consider the postage time and the time for the salespeople to reach the prospect by phone, you could be talking about a 14-day or more delay between the prospect responding and being contacted. In 14 days customer interest could wane. They might have already bought from the competitor! *The solution: shorten the time between receiving leads and contacting customers whenever possible.*

Why do they call prospects only after receiving responses? They could call every prospect three days after the mailing or email to explain their service in more depth. This would generate substantially more appointments. Some companies generate as much as eight times as many appointments using this system. Naturally this costs more due to telephone charges and staff time. A financial return against investment could easily be calculated to help them decide whether to call all prospects or just those who respond.

The management strategy to cure this company of its 60% lost business ratio and create a 150% increase in sales should be:

THE RIGHT WAY

1. Cut the time for response to leads to one day.
2. Incorporate a daily tracking sheet listing all prospects. The sales force can use this as a working tool.
3. Have daily follow-up calendars used by each member of the sales force to record those who need to be called.
4. Prepare a weekly activity summary sheet listing calls and results.
5. Develop a similar results report with monthly totals.

Tracking systems are essential to management and salespeople alike. A good system once adopted is appreciated for the self-discipline it imposes on everyone. It should be simple use and easy to understand by those who review it.

PUT EVERY LEAD INTO THE SYSTEM

1. Track Exhibition and Advertising Leads

I remember watching a marketing manager come into the office after an exhibition. He reached into his pocket, pulled out a handful of business cards, and threw them on the sales secretary's desk. "Ann, here are the exhibition leads," he said. He never spoke to the Sales Manager.

Two months later the sales manager asked Ann, "Where are those leads from the exhibition?" That's the way leads passed from marketing to sales. Most of the prospects had already spent their money elsewhere. This sad but true story repeats itself too often.

When advertising or an exhibition is done, leads are generated. The same tracking system can be used or a similar one developed. The important thing is that *each* inquiry enters the system and is followed up *quickly*.

Companies spend vast sums for exhibition stands, yet follow-up is often left to the discretion of each member of the sales force. Many times salespeople are pressed for time due to sales commitments prior to and following the exhibition. Cards collected at exhibitions but never entered into the system don't create sales.

Unless someone is specifically responsible for exhibition follow-up, this is exactly what can happen. Why not appoint someone from inside or outside the sales force to be responsible for getting the inquiries into the system? After all, the lead is as good as gold. Why not put someone in charge of it? Once in the system, the leads can be followed up in the normal way.

2. Track Non-Sales Department Leads

Another area of potential lost sales for companies is the inquiry picked up outside the sales department. It could be a telephone call answered by the security guard, the passing production engineer, or the switchboard. Therefore, everyone in a company needs to become aware of the existence of the tracking system and the importance of getting the lead into the system.

But knowledge alone won't save leads. The best system we've seen is one in which a central person is designated as the lead coordinator. This person can have the responsibility of entering leads into the system on a daily basis, whether they come in by telephone, through production, or on a scrap of paper from a cocktail party. All conventional and unconventional leads should go into the system.

3. Keep a Phone Log

Remember Dave Goillon's engineers who were mentioned earlier? Why not keep a call-in pad by the phone in every department to record names and phone numbers of prospects.

At my company we keep a phone call-in book at each telephone. Later someone switches the relevant inquiry information to the tracking system. By recording each call we also get the spin-off benefit of being able to refer back to anyone who called, the date, their phone number, and so on.

How effective is your lead tracking and conversion system, and how does it compare to those of other companies? Give yourself a 10 out of 10 if:

1. You can immediately put your hands on a list of all conventional and unconventional inquiries in one place, kept for easy access and tracking. This can be a central place for each member of the sales team;
2. All inquiries are duplicated in a master file for current and future reference;
3. A calendarized tracking system records each *future* action for each prospect and the date it is to be taken;
4. Management gets a regular breakdown of the activities and results of each member of the sales team;
5. Management studies the activity details regularly and takes corrective action before problems occur.

If your systems aren't as airtight as you would like, don't despair. But take action now to correct them. The results will surprise you.

They surprised Phil Parker. He was on the sales desk of a financial futures trading company. After coming on one of our seminars, the first action he took was to start a lead tracking system.

The course finished on June 7. On June 8, a colleague of Phil's gave him a lead. He called and found out that the prospect was on vacation but would be back on June 23. He entered the name into his new lead tracking system, indicating action on June 23. Then a series of conversations ensued, in fact nine carefully followed up phone calls over the next nine weeks. They were all duly noted in Phil's lead tracking system.

Suddenly in the tenth week, on September 8, exactly three months after his first call, Phil got a call. It was the prospect, this time calling Phil. He said, "I'm ready to order."

"Without the system," Phil told me, "I might have called once or twice, but over a three-month period I would have forgotten the client. I used to enter the prospect names in my diary. BUT when the page was turned, the prospect was forgotten."

The important thing is that with a system like Phil's, *you are in control.* Your effort is documented and logged. You know exactly where you stand with each prospect.

What if someone in Phil's position had started 10, 20, or 50 clients, and after a few calls, given them up? There would be enormous wasted effort. Why not make your effort *really* count?

Now you have food for thought. The sooner you get an effective system, the sooner your results will increase.

EFFECTIVE TRACKING SYSTEMS

Effective systems rely on three things:

1. The system: It must be good and easy to use.
2. The management of the system: Someone needs to coordinate and monitor the carry through.
3. The lead coordinator: One person needs to be responsible for putting leads into the system.

If you want to improve your own performance independent of others, you will have to carry out all three tasks yourself. It will be worth it. You'll feel much more in control of your activities and your results will go up dramatically.

What if you're reading this book but you're not in sales? The same system can be used for achieving any goal.

When Bill and I were collaborating on this book, I realized that we only had three months left to complete it. I wanted time to do four rewrites of each chapter. With over 20 chapters and four rewrites, that meant nearly 100 days were needed.

As three months have only 90 days, we were already pressed. I solved the problem by reallocating the time, giving me more time for the first draft of each chapter, and less time for rewrite touch-ups. We made our deadline because I created a tracking system for what had to be done each day.

But I know why many people miss deadlines. If I hadn't applied my business knowledge and practiced what I preached, I would have missed mine too. No matter what your goal is, use a tracking system. Know how much you have to accomplish each day.

Remember to stop losing business needlessly:

Develop an airtight tracking system.

ACTION SHEET
Chapter 12

Ideas for Development:

1. Come to terms with the fact that leads are like gold and should be handled as pedantically as the company's money is handled..
2. Develop an action provoking system that tracks both conventional and unconventional leads.
3. Analyze the weaknesses of your current system of following up on leads.
4. Create sales management control of leads just as you have financial controls of money.
5. Make sure every lead enters the system.
6. List other points here:
7.
8.

Of the above ideas, which one is likely to yield the best results?

What percentage of sales (or performance) increase could realistically be expected?

How long would it take: to develop the idea? to get results?

Who would have to be involved?

What date should we start?

What is the first step I should take?

Chapter 13

The Make or Break Buying Period

How long does it take for customers to decide whether or not to buy a product? In retail, a customer may make the decision to buy a cosmetic in three minutes. In aerospace the decision could take three years or more and involve several layers of decision making.

We call the time period between customer awareness of the product and their decision the critical 'make or break' buying period. The reason that this period is critical is that we can make or break our chances of selling during that period by our actions.

What is the average buying decision period for your product? Every company has an average customer buying cycle. This period varies among industries.

DON'T DENY YOUR CUSTOMER BUYING CYCLE

I know many salespeople who deny that an average period can be determined. They reason that each customer is different and by denying there is a critical period, they put their energy into the sale too late. This weakens their effectiveness. They neglect doing the appropriate things while the customer's interest is the highest, and they therefore lose the business. Instead, they concentrate energy on the period when customer interest is waning, causing frustration for themselves, their company, and their customer. In fact, 80% of ineffective salespeople put their energy in at this stage. Don't let this happen to you and your people.

Figure 1 below shows the customer buying cycle.

Much of the success in selling our ideas or our product does, in fact, come down to taking the right action at the right time.

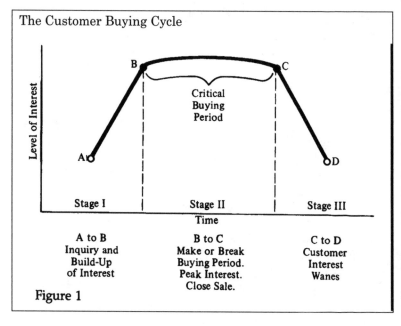

Figure 1

Stage I

You'll see that Stage I is the period of the inquiry when the customer's interest starts to be enticed.

Stage II

During Stage II of the buying cycle, the customer's interest is at its peak. This interest usually occurs during your presentation or the demonstration of the product. Sometimes it lasts until shortly afterwards. If we take the right action then, we will make the sale.

Stage III

Customers' interest can only last so long. Other things can come in the way. Competitors can come along, doubts can build in their mind, or other priorities can come up. When interest starts to wane like this, we are in Stage III of the buying cycle.

DON'T PUT YOUR EFFORT IN TOO LATE

Top class salespeople or business executives—ones who are respected for their success by their peers and community-- know that action needs to be taken quickly. In selling, they will put their emphasis at Stage II, when interest is at its peak. They know that they themselves must instigate the action and not wait.

However, it's easier to procrastinate, hoping problems will solve themselves, hoping sales will evolve by themselves. They don't, of course, and then people find themselves putting energy into the sale too late.

This kind of thinking is the sign of ineffectiveness. It's the sign of people not being honest with themselves. So we can say that self-deception is the root of losing business needlessly.

Why else do people not take appropriate action during the critical buying period? The three most common reasons are:

1. Fear
2. Insufficient training or skill
3. Lack of management discipline or motivation

If we have fear of answering objections during the presentation, the customers go away not fully understanding our product or services.

If we have fear of asking directly for a decision or commitment, it would be because we haven't developed a comfortable way of doing it. Then fear and insufficient methods both keep us from taking the right action at the right time. The problem could be the lack of management skills. In this case even the best salespeople can periodically lose motivation.

STOP FEAR AND IMPROVE YOUR TRAINING METHODS

Let's take the case of fear of asking directly for a decision or commitment. This is an area that plagues most people, but can be easily overcome with a step-by-step questioning process.

Most people steer away from asking for the order because it sounds too direct. If the customer says, "No," it's too final. But we can ask for the order gradually without risk. The key is to work simply in small stages towards agreement.

I first became aware of the forcefulness of this process when a company president complimented me for asking him, "Does this seem like the kind of thing you're looking for?" He felt it was not offensive and yet to the point.

Other simple questions serve the same purpose. We can all learn from each other and build up a repertoire of inoffensive and effective questions.

I remember listening to one of our own clients, Michael Campbell when we were on a sales call in Cairo. After our introductions he opened his questioning by very simply asking, "What would you be looking for from a supplier?" With that one simple question he was able to learn a tremendous amount about the customer's needs. This was the start of his closing process. Next, he went on to prove he could meet those needs.

A good opening question like the one above, leads us easily to our close. For example, "John, earlier you mentioned you want reliability, quick delivery, and a product that does this and that. Since ours offers these benefits and others, would you be able to add our name to the suppliers list?"

"When would the next request for quotation come up?"

"Do you have an requirements at the moment that we can satisfy?"

It's essential to increase our 'questioning' options for getting customer approval. This helps to overcome the fear people have of direct questioning.

IMPROVE MANAGEMENT DISCIPLINE AND MOTIVATION

What about management discipline and motivation as it relates to the critical buying period? Doesn't it make sense to keep our people focused on the 'critical buying period'? When we help them put their energy into Stage II, the peak buying period, they increase their returns. The company gains and they gain. Their motivation continues to go up, and so do their results.

Some companies keep their salespeople informed of the cost of sales development in order to demonstrate their support. Each week, when the responses come in, all costs are added up and divided by the number of responses.

The sales force is made aware of the urgency to act quickly in order to reinforce this expenditure. They realize that if the expenditure were stopped, the only alternative would be cold calling. The time and frustration needed to cold-call takes valuable time away from face-to-face selling, which means fewer sales.

The realization of the cost of sales support will cause you to follow up on all sales activities during the critical buying period.

Knowing the cost of lead generation won't help everyone's motivation, but it won't hurt. You know your people and you know everyone needs to be motivated differently.

When you run a tighter ship, success breeds success.

I always think of my good friend Lady Peggy Lindsay who makes her point about management practices more vivid by saying that, "Some efforts taken at the wrong time are as useless as pushing water uphill with a rake. It's certainly true of the Stage III buying cycle. Putting effort into the close too late--by waiting until interest has started to wane--is like pushing water uphill with a rake!

Remember to stop losing business needlessly.

Don't let opportunities slip through your fingers. Strike while the iron is hot in the peak buying period.

ACTION SHEET
Chapter 13

Ideas for Development:

1. Determine the average time of the buying cycle for your product.
2. Make sure the order is asked for during the peak interest period.
3. When action is not taken during the peak interest period, determine the cause: fear, insufficient training or skill, lack of discipline and motivation.
4. Develop and practice excellent openings and closings.
5. Communicate the cost of generating leads and sales support given to the sales force.
6. List other points here:
7.
8.

Of the above ideas, which one is likely to yield the best results?

What percentage of sales (or performance) increase could realistically be expected?

How long would it take: to develop the idea? to get results?

Who would have to be involved?

What date should we start?

What is the first step I should take?

Chapter 14

How to Cure Follow-Up Complacency

Would anyone miss a sale purposely? Of course not.

Yet, when any of us look back at the sales we've lost, we sometimes see what actions we should have taken. We could have acted faster, or we could have said something a better way.

TAKE PREVENTATIVE MEASURES

Why not then, take action ahead of time that will help to prevent us from slipping into this complacency mold next time? The real way to cure follow-up complacency is to carry out the sales process effectively at all stages. Then follow-up becomes less of a problem.

What is your sales closing ratio--that is, what percentage of business do you actually acquire from the total initial inquiries? Could you do better? If so, what would this increase mean to you personally, to your future, to your company?

In this chapter we'll show you three foolproof, easy-to-use measures that can dramatically increase your closing ratio. It's proven to work with people in companies of all sizes and all industries.

MEASURE I: DEVELOP YOUR OPTIONS
INCREASING YOUR CLOSING RATIO

With your incentive in mind let's look at nine options for increasing our closing rate.

The following nine options, when practiced, acquired and applied, give practical ways to express your ideas with the impact and influence needed to sell.

1. Paint a Mental Picture

Tell a story that involves the prospect--one in which they can see themselves using, benefiting from, and enjoying our product or service.

Let's say that we know from previous discussions that our prospect, John Jones, is under pressure to double the sales of his department next year and is thinking of using our seminars for in-house training.

So we might say, "When you use our service we know you want to be sure you get immediate results. The way we help people get immediate results is to have them estimate the percentage increase in sales they will get from each section." They also make an implementation plan. This means they've taken the first step during the seminar.

Imagine yourself as manager, being part of the planning process, with full commitment from your team. Imagine the feeling of confidence and control you'll have knowing each step that will be taken to reach each goal, so that you can monitor the achievement and make policy adjustments as you go. You'll be able to sleep at night knowing exactly where you stand.

The prospect can then see himself using, benefiting, and enjoying our service. What mental picture can you give of your product or service that uses these three points?

2. Use Analogies

I once heard a man interviewed on the radio who spent 15 minutes going from one analogy to the next.

Analogies take practice, but once you've mastered them, they can be very effective. Practice by choosing any item in the room. Then tie it to your product, idea, or service. "See that filing cabinet over there? In some ways it's like the steady, controlled growth you want for your company. You don't want to open the drawer one year and find it full, the next year empty. It's like the factory floor, you want it full at all times." Practice analogies everywhere you go--in the car, while you walk, everywhere.

3. Show Referral Letters

Personalized referral letters that address specific issues are wonderful swayer of opinion, especially if they are genuinely honest and *specific*.

They are even more effective if they mention problems that were amicably resolved. We find that eight out of ten companies overlook the benefit of reference letters or are reluctant to ask for them. But, what if they could honestly say to a prospect, "I just had a letter in today from a client who had your same concern, which we satisfied." If you want to increase sales you have to be open minded to all ideas.

Why not develop a simple and non-embarrassing way of asking for reference letters? You might say, "John, what did you find beneficial or unique about your product or service?" And then ask if they would be kind enough to jot it down in their own words for you. Don't ask for the letter first. Ask for their opinion first. Then your job is easier.

Reference letters serve two purposes. First, they convince others of our reliability because a third party is more believable than our own stories. Second, when people record their commendation in writing, it confirms it in their own mind. Therefore, they are more likely to remain customers and refer others, than if they don't write.

4. Quote Facts and Figures

Statistics give people a feeling of having a grip on solid facts. If you're using figures in writing, you'll want to note the difference between the written and the numerical form and the impact it makes on the reader. Which catches the eye first? Which gives a solid impression? You can write forty percent, 40% or 40 percent. All give a different impression.

Try to quote the source, because the statistic has even more impact and credibility. An example might be: "Today, over 60% of the families in the US own their own home, according to Federal Reserve Board figures." Because you are told the source, aren't you more likely to believe it? Most people are.

5. Quote Satisfied Customers

Quote satisfied customers, and be specific. "John Smith in Pasadena used our Machine 308 and he called to tell us that after three months his running cost savings paid for the machine! Naturally you follow it with a question: "Would this kind of saving be a help to you?"

6. Use Demonstrators

Nothing is more alive than the real thing. People buy with all their senses, not just their logical, analytical brain. A demonstration allows them to see and touch the product.

If you have two computer salespeople, and one brings a video of the machine, and the other brings the real thing, who wins? Usually the live machine demonstration because people love to touch and hold, to experiment, to do it themselves.

What if you're in the service industry? Think about all angles you can use. Once I was doing a series of in-house seminars with the Lloyd's Financial Futures people. On the first seminar, I did not suggest they use demonstrations because I couldn't think of what they could do until they invited me down to the trading floor. Then I realized how beneficial it would be for their client to witness the service and see the benefits they would be getting from having traders on the floor.

Be inventive. Don't close your mind to these ideas. With a little ingenuity you can apply all these methods to your own business and increase your results.

7. Quote Authorities

Quoting an authority or an expert in the field endorses a product. We buy it more readily. This has proven itself in advertising consumer items. And it works just as convincingly in large scale industrial items. "The President of XYZ Company uses our products." What authority can you quote?

8. Use Written Material

The written word can be more convincing than the spoken word and appeals to people's visual senses. Literature, brochures, fact sheets and web sites all serve this purpose. It's important that the written copy be as neat and professional as possible. All written material should state benefits as well as features. Charts, graphs, indented written format, all help to give it variety and reader appeal. So do photographs.

9. Use Samples

Supplying a sample of the product promotes customer appeal. This is simple if the product is as small as a sugar cube. But what if it's bigger or more expensive?

What about a replica of the product? John Ryan had a photographic replica made of his company's ammeter. It's small enough to fit in an envelope. The inside of the leaflet lists the benefits and features. The back suggests a demonstration and has a space for the agent's address details.

It also mentions the company's other products. That's a lot of information to pack into an eight-inch by three-inch paper replica. The cut out folded version is an irresistible 'touch me.'

Obviously a real sample is preferable. But if that's not possible, be inventive as John has, and save the sample for the demonstration.

BECOME SKILLED AT NINE METHODS

Use all of the nine alternatives listed above for expressing your ideas in a way that influences decisions. By developing them now, isn't it easier to use it when you need it? I'll never forget the plight of a management consultant I visited some time ago who had never had any sales training. He wanted to arrange a meeting with a large prospective client company. He called them and said simply "John Jones is in town. We thought you might like to come over while he's here." He didn't give any enticements. What impact would he have made using one of the nine illustrative methods--perhaps a verbal picture to motivate the buyer, perhaps a demonstration offer or a quote from a satisfied customer, perhaps sending literature or documentation ahead.

Next time you pick up the phone or go into a meeting, ask yourself what incentive you're offering the others for seeing things from your point of view.

The nine methods will help you. What closing ratio of convincing people do you have now? Why not measure your ability to convince others with each meeting or phone call, by using the nine methods?

MEASURE II: USE AN ACTION PROMPTING SYSTEM

Not only do we need to say the right thing, we have to say it at the right time. We need a system for follow up that is painless, that doesn't need thought to get started. It needs to be like a revolving wheel--once started, it carries you with it.

We've developed an internal system for sales follow-up that many of our clients have adopted. It's simple and so effective that we use a similar system for other office activities.

There are many systems available. Most people will use a computerized system, but a manual system can work just as well for some people. In our system, we keep track of clients to call back, or confirmation letters to be sent with the exact date that the action needs to be taken. Make sure that when you open the page for the day, or see the screen, all actions to be taken that day are displayed.

One of our management trainees, Josef Rutzel, even used it in his personal life. When Josef went back to Wuerzburg, Germany, he scheduled his athletics, his hobbies, his friends, and his thesis writing. He says that the system makes him twice as productive.

Rob Mann manages his exports with a system like this to monitor and control call-in inquiries. The company has always sent literature promptly. Now they can follow up systematically. The management controls created from a system like this, bring peace of mind.

MEASURE III: DISPLAY THE RESULTS FOR EVERYONE TO SEE

The last step in the chain required to cure complacency is to publicize results--not just sales results. Publicize everything. Show how many calls were made. Tell how many calls resulted in conversation! Report how many appointments were made. How many sales were made. How it compares to last week, last month.

Chart it, graph it, publicize it. Everybody needs to feel someone recognizes their achievement. They need to follow their own progress as well. Give it drama. Give it variety. Use bar graphs, line graphs, and dot graphs.

Have you heard the story of the great steel tycoon who used to walk through the factory and mark a chalk number on the floor? Each shift finally realized the number referred to the previous shift's productivity. Soon they were marking their own chalk number and each was higher than the last. When we give people recognition, it inspires action.

Remember to stop losing business needlessly:

Take preventative medicine;
Do the right thing, at the right time; and
Display the results.

ACTION SHEET
Chapter 14

Ideas for Development:

1. Develop skills in painting a mental picture using analogies and quoting facts and figures.
2. Quote satisfied customers and authorities; show referral letters and written material.
3. Give demonstrations and use samples.
4. Have a good action prompting system.
5. Display the results for all to see.
6. List other points here:
7.
8.

Of the above ideas, which one is likely to yield the best results?

What percentage of sales (or performance) increase could realistically be expected?

How long would it take: to develop the idea? to get results?

Who would have to be involved?

What date should we start?

What is the first step I should take?

Chapter 15

Personality Profiles:
How To Work with Them

"No matter what I say, I don't seem to be able to get through. Why won't they decide to buy or not? They have all the facts, the best price, the fastest delivery--why won't they make a decision?" Does this sound familiar?

Business is lost needlessly every day by managers and salespeople who haven't learned to adapt to personality profiles.

When two personalities come together in a room, it's a little like two chemicals coming together in a test tube. Each one affects the other. We wouldn't put two chemicals together in a test tube without knowing the properties of each! The reaction could be explosive.

Yet we often throw ourselves into situations with other people without knowing the properties of each--the personality make-up of them, or of ourselves. No wonder the outcome is less than perfect.

Imagine the following scenario, a true story related by Bill at a seminar. Behind the desk sits a conservatively dressed buyer, with neat appearance, white shirt, dark suit and tie. His desk is clear, with a white note pad, neatly headed with the meeting date and title, placed carefully on the middle of the desk.

The salesman enters, bright red tie, and matching silk handkerchief showing flamboyantly from the pocket of his expensive suit, designer briefcase, and a gold bracelet dangling at the cuff of the silk shirt. He exudes an enthusiastic "Good Morning."

Did the two characters hit it off immediately? No, the salesman, not trained in responding differently to each personality type, failed to notice the hesitant reaction from the buyer. The desk chair moving further away, the reluctance to answer questions, the softening tone of his voice, were all clues to the buyer's personality.

What did the salesman do? He moved forward when the buyer withdrew, he asked more questions when the buyer hesitated. He raised his voice as the buyer lowered his. And so it went. The salesman responded in ways he knew best. The more aggressive he became, the more the buyer retreated. The salesman was losing business needlessly.

BUILD TRUST THROUGH COMPATIBILITY

Had he been a student of personalities, he would have known he needed to respond more like the other person to build compatibility. Without compatibility a relationship can't begin to grow. We need to show compatibility first. Later we can show our differences and strengthen our relationship. But first there needs to be common ground.

Everyone needs to feel there are compatible areas before they accept the differences. Shouldn't we all remember to respond in an acceptable way to our buyer the next time we're selling an idea or a product?

To be successful, we have to be adaptable. When dealing with conservative or analytical buyers, salespeople need to present the facts of the case and then back off, taking care to set a time and date for a follow-up call and religiously keeping to that appointment. This type of analytical, fact-finding buyer will resent any early intrusion into their world, unless it is at their invitation, and on their time and terms. In order to stop losing business needlessly, we must foster that compatibility.

The successful salesperson will recognize these personality signals and treat each sales situation differently. They will watch for the signs and signals from the prospect. They will adapt their style to build compatibility.

DON'T LET ASSUMPTIONS KILL THE SALE

One of Bill's closest colleagues, Norman Berry, decided to apply his hard work and integrity ethics to starting two new companies. One was a distribution company for security and safes.

On one sales call, he was faced with a husband and wife buying team, who owned a lock and safe store. The husband liked Norman and loved to talk. Norman discussed the business with him at first. The wife was more task minded. He checked and cross-checked the problems and the recent sales trends with her.

After understanding the buying motives, Norman turned to the wife and said, "I understand you've already sold one floor safe this week, and had another inquiry yesterday. How about taking the three I have in the car? With the price reductions I've calculated, you should be able to sell those by the time I'm around next week."

The sale was his. The order was signed by the wife. Norman knew that the husband was the one person not to sell to--conversations with him revealed buying motives, but when it came to getting the order, the wife was the task minded decision maker.

Many sales, and hours, have been lost by salespeople who don't understand the personalities of the buying duo. If we presume that one person is the decision-maker without looking deeper, we may be wasting our time.

Personalities complement each other, and we need to direct our efforts properly to each.

ESTABLISH THE KEY MOTIVATORS, DON'T GUESS

An article in Psychology Today, expressed the idea that the sales profession is a psychological laboratory. It involves testing human intelligence, persistence, persuasiveness, and resilience, plus the ability to deal with rejection on a daily basis.

In the consulting field, Bill's company, Sykes Consultants, uses a personality profile predictor to screen and understand people's personal characteristics. As a qualified analyst using uses a personality profile predictor to screen and understand this type of predictor, Bill is able to develop personality profiles of individuals who are likely to succeed in certain types of jobs.

In sales and management jobs, it's particularly important to find out how certain types of people will interface with their own salespeople and with potential customers. The profiles also show how the personalities of individuals will interface.

Isn't it better to find out from testing rather than to spend a lifetime guessing. Sales managers, and indeed all company directors, need to recognize the styles and talents that are inherent in their successful salespeople. How else can they motivate their people to achieve the best results?

Guessing at what motivates people can lead to disaster. Studies consistently show that different motives drive top salespeople to success. Some of these factors includes the need for status, control, respect, routine, accomplishment, stimulation, and honesty. Is that what you would have guessed about salespeople who achieve success?

The Psychology Today article indicates that many of the best salespeople seek recognition as proof of their ability. They enjoy being with people and delight in influencing them. They need respect and want to be seen as experts on what is right, best, or appropriate.

And, contrary to the common stereotype, most like routine and don't like having it interrupted. They need accomplishment, not just material comforts. After a while material rewards lose their ability to motivate.

Many like to create new challenges such as going after impossible sales. They make the impossible happen. They thrive on challenge and welcome outside stimulation to channel their high level of energy.

Many have a strong need to believe in their product and service support. Their inner need for honesty means that they will switch jobs if the company reputation falls or the product quality declines.

Understanding personality profiles, either through testing or simply by studying people's needs, is vital. If we are going to influence, coach, and motivate our team into a dynamic sales force, or to sell our product and ideas, then we need to understand each and every person. For, indeed, they are all different. They are all individuals with separate values and needs.

Remember, the buyer holds the order pad! Don't forget the red-tie salesman who advanced as the buyer withdrew. Don't follow in his footsteps. If you want to succeed, take your cue from the successful. Join the superstars of sales who know that their selling style must be adapted to suit each individual buyer. It is up to the salesperson to do the adapting and not the buyer.

Remember to stop losing business needlessly:

Recognize personality styles and adapt to it.

ACTION SHEET
Chapter 15

Ideas for Development:

1. Realize that each prospect needs to be sold to differently.
2. Build trust through compatibility.
3. Don't jump to conclusions about who the decision maker is before analyzing the personalities.
4. Consider a personality profiling tool to learn about yourself or your sales team.
5. To motivate a sales team or a customer, consider personality differences.
6. List other points here:
7.
8.

Of the above ideas, which one is likely to yield the best results?

What percentage of sales (or performance) increase could realistically be expected?

How long would it take: to develop the idea? to get results?

Who would have to be involved?

What date should we start?

What is the first step I should take?

PART 6

How To Analyze Your Current Situation And Develop Areas Of Improvement

Chapter 16

Sales Literature: Does It Sell or Tell?

What areas of your literature could be updated to increase your sales returns? One UK company found out the hard way. Because they had never previously sold overseas, they had no need to put 'England' on their address--only the city and county.

One day after visiting the US to generate business the owner discovered he had missed out on a large bid. He could easily have won, if his address had been complete. The American customer simply created the request for quotation exactly as he had it--city and county, no country. The envelope worked its way through the international mail network and landed on his desk a day after the closing date of the bid! A sadder director we have never seen.

The point is that many things about sales literature leave much to be desired. Not only are addresses incomplete--often features and benefits are unclear. Customers jump to the conclusion that the product is less effective than the competitor's product.

Sales literature is fundamental to all business activities. It is often the first contact that the customer has with the company. It represents the company, its products, its philosophy, and its attitude to the customer.

Are you doing all you can to enhance this valuable way of communicating with your customer? Are you making sure that your literature sells? If we expect to generate business, we have to tell our prospects how they can benefit by using our products. It's not enough just to list features. Features tell, they don't sell.

DEVELOP A CHECKLIST

Let's look at some of the problems relating to sales literature, and ways of overcoming them quickly and cost effectively.

- Is the wording of our sales literature or web sites prepared by people with sales expertise who know how to state benefits clearly?

- Is the wording adequate for every level of decision-maker, including technical, non-technical, and financial managers?

- Does it include a clear and easy way to respond? Does it include a clear, full address including the country, if our work is international? A clearly marked telephone number, department to be contacted, or, better yet, an easy-to-use reply section?

Reflect on the importance of stating features and benefits as discussed in earlier chapters. Also, remember that the human mind is not capable of retaining information for long. People forget 80% of what they hear within two days. Therefore, sales literature should be used to jog the memory and to explain the benefits of your product in depth.

TAKE CORRECTIVE ACTION QUICKLY

If your literature currently doesn't meet the above criteria, you are losing business needlessly. A separate sales sheet can be produced to supplement the technical literature quickly and easily. A company we know that makes industrial machinery had a very technical, fact-filled piece of literature. It listed only features, no benefits. They therefore produced a single sheet that fit inside their folded leaflet. It listed their five primary features in short bold headings, followed by the benefits in italic style print. They gave the address and telephone contact at the bottom with a ruled line around it which made it stand out very effectively.

Whether you want to produce a separate sales sheet such as this or redesign your literature altogether, remember: The purpose of literature is to let the customers know what the product is and how it will benefit them, thus enticing their interest and refreshing their memories each time they read it.

GIVE BENEFITS AND ENTICEMENTS

- Be sure to state the benefits--how the customer will gain from using your product or service;

- Give proof and evidence of its quality and benefits. Show referral letters, news clippings, statistics. Give facts, quote experts, customers, and so on;

- Use enticement--give reasons that persuade customers to contact you now while their interest is high -- limited time offers, samples offers, or an extra giveaway with the product;

- State your address and contact point clearly and completely.

If you want to improve your returns, take corrective action quickly on your sales literature and web sites. It can be fast, easy, and cost effective.

Remember to develop areas of improvement:

Make sure your sales literature sells the benefits as well as the features.

ACTION SHEET
Chapter 16

Ideas for Development:

1. Develop a checklist of necessary points to be included in sales literature and web sites.
2. Make sure your wording is appropriate for every level of decision making.
3. Include benefits and enticements, even in technical literature.
4. Provide an easy way to respond.
5. Take corrective action with supplemental pages to cure inadequacies.
6. List other points here:
7.
8.

Of the above ideas, which one is likely to yield the best results?

What percentage of sales (or performance) increase could realistically be expected?

How long would it take: to develop the idea? to get results?

Who would have to be involved?

What date should we start?

What is the first step I should take?

Chapter 17

A 15-Point Checklist for Evaluating Sales Presentations

Mark McConnel was in his early 50s when appointed to takeover the reins of a subsidiary of a large computer service company. He had 15 years management experience with the company and before his appointment had been in charge of everything except sales and marketing. He knew the customers and the service inside out and seemed well qualified to head the company.

The first 18 months proved worrisome to the parent company and eventually to Mark. He knew sales were rocky under his new sales manager, but he couldn't quite get a grip on it.

The parent company could. They saw that Mark was leaving too much authority in the hands of the new sales manager, without the controls, checks, and balances which he used so successfully in running other facets of the company.

During these first 18 months there was a personnel turnover in sales of 52 people in an attempt to keep a steady team of 10.

No wonder Mark's ulcers flared and the parent company grew cautious. Was it Mark's fault? Yes. Unfortunately, he just didn't know what to look for, what to believe or not to believe. If the sales manager and the marketing manager had two different stories, he had to support one or the other on trust rather than experience and knowledge.

TOP MANAGERS NEED SALES ACUMEN TOO

Mark realized, after coaching from HQ, that he needed to gain sales acumen. He needed to know the right questions to ask. He needed to know the difference between good and bad sales presentations so that he could judge the sales team's capability and not be putty in the hands of the sales manager.

He also needed, as head of the company, to be able to give a decent sales presentation himself from time to time when the situation called for it.

At first Mark was hesitant to get involved. He thought salespeople were born as salespeople and that he would never be one. He thought he should be able to leave sales in the hands of others who were hired for the job.

Finally, after a year and a half of chaos, the parent company gave Mark a do-or-die ultimatum. They insisted that he observe their best sales personnel until he learned the tricks of the trade.

Mark was lucky. He survived the ordeal. They eventually removed the sales manager and put Mark in direct charge of the sales force for a period while he gained valuable hands-on experience.

He learned that salespeople are made, not born. He learned how to evaluate good and bad performance. He was lucky during those months of trial and tribulation that he had an already established customer base to rely on. Without that established customer base, things would have been even worse.

Many corporate directors express uneasiness about understanding the sales side of their business. When it comes to product design, production, or finance, they know where and how to lead the company.

When it comes to sales, these directors are less confident. They feel there are too many unscientific parameters.

Often the same is true of small company owners. They need sales knowledge to lead their company into growth from day one. This is a key ingredient in getting a new company off the ground.

REALIZE THAT THE WHOLE IS
THE SUM OF THE PARTS

The checklist that follows was designed for companies, large and small. The checklist can be used as a management control sheet.

Therefore, when using the checklist, remind yourself that you are looking at a series of ingredients. If you are going to perform at top efficiency, all the ingredients must be in place. If they are not, your performance sputters and spurts and sometimes comes to a complete halt. If you identify which ingredients need attention early enough, you can avoid coming to a standstill.

The checklist allows quick and easy assessment of performance so that help can be given to each individual in the area of current weakness. We all fluctuate on our strengths and weaknesses.

The purpose of this monitoring is to spot current weaknesses and correct them swiftly so that the company can move ahead quickly. We want to increase the momentum of sales.

Just as doing the wrong thing in production can ruin the product, so can doing the wrong thing in sales, ruin sales momentum. Score yourself or others on a 1–10 scale and then decide what training or disciplines need to be put into place.

To use the checklist most effectively, consider:

1. Which points meet high standards?

2. Which points need training or stronger control?

3. Ways you can support good performance as well as ways you can train and motivate in areas of weakness.

Criteria for Evaluating Effective Sales Presentations

Points to Check (for Myself and Other Members of Staff)	Level of Proficiency (1-10)	Needs Training (Yes/No)	Ways We Can Support Others and Train Ourselves

• Prepared ahead
   • papers
   • examples, demonstrations			

• Knows product			
• Presents features			
• Presents benefits			
• Finds out which benefit the customer wants "Dominant Buying Motive"			
• Tells only important benefits			
• Handles fear vs. confidence on objectives			
• Can make point in two minutes on phone			
• Makes point in 17 minutes in person			
• Recognizes emotional needs of customer			
• Recognizes logical needs of customer			
• Follows up on time			
• Has a follow-up system of control			
• Gets commitments			
• Asks for orders			

Remember to analyze your current situation:

Use the 15-point checklist to evaluate and improve all sales presentations.

ACTION SHEET
Chapter 17

Ideas for Development:

1. If you are in operations or finance, gain sales acumen now in order to prepare for the future.
2. Get hands on experience by accompanying sales personnel whenever possible.
3. Remember that the sales process is a series of ingredients, just as production and finance are.
4. Use the checklist to evaluate yourself and others.
5. Plan training to raise the bar on weak areas.
6. List other points here:
7.
8.

Of the above ideas, which one is likely to yield the best results?

What percentage of sales (or performance) increase could realistically be expected?

How long would it take: to develop the idea? to get results?

Who would have to be involved?

What date should we start?

What is the first step I should take?

Chapter 18

How to Recognize
Sales Force Needs
... and Meet Them Cost Effectively

Jean Morgan-Bryant runs her own company, and after only six years in business, she won one of the top awards for export achievement. As export merchants, Jean's people are on duty seven days a week, 52 weeks a year. They take calls for orders on Saturdays, on Christmas and holidays, just like any other day. Their customers in the Middle East and Asia operate on different time zones and different holidays, and want to find the Morgan Bryant people at work, available when they need them.

Obviously Jean's people have met the challenge of long hours, high performance, and dedication to the job. Not many companies win the coveted export award.

And obviously Jean has met the challenge of recognizing the needs of her sales force. What methods does she use to inspire this dedication and high performance?

PERSONAL ATTENTION GETS RESULTS

Jean's answer is 'personal attention to everyone's needs.' Jean started with two people. In those days she did all the selling and all the customer liaison. By the time they won the award, the company had a staff of 28. Jean had to 'transfer' her knowledge, her inspiration, and her skill to all 28 people over that period.

"I used to sit at each sales desk, and show each person exactly how to handle customers." She still does it on occasion, when her managers are away. "People learn best and are motivated best by personal attention," says Jean.

What about the time that this personal attention takes? Can it be cost effective? Jean believes emphatically that, "If we train people properly, they can become a real resource."

What did Jean have in mind about training people properly? She gave me the following example. In the early days of the company, she had a young man working for her who was bright, dedicated, and good with customers.

He had only one weakness--numbers. "Who doesn't have weaknesses?" thought Jean. "We'll train him to use numbers better and he'll be a real asset to the company." Sounds sensible? To Jean it did.

In most situations, people not as optimistic as Jean might have been more doubtful. Numbers were an essential part of the business. Pricing, shipping, import duties--they all relied on numbers. Should Jean really spend her time with him, or should she look for someone with people skills and number skills?

No, attitude was more important to Jean than skill. Skill could be taught with the right patience and training. What was the outcome? The employee learned to work with numbers fast. His dedication remained. So did his skill with people. Jean was right, he did become 'a real asset to the company' as she predicted. His skills continued to increase and eventually he became a director of the company.

Needs Are Individualistic

Everyone needs something different in order to become a top performer. Some need specific training as this young man did. Others need motivation, in ways as specific as this man needed training.

Skill areas that need attention are usually easy to spot. Motivational areas are not as easy. Often we think we know, but we find out later that we didn't.

What do you think is the biggest motivator for people? Most think it's a high salary. I thought that was true until I read reports showing that pay ranked only third in people's order of priority.

The fundamental truth is that people are looking for something else besides pay as a motivator. The first and second ranking motivators are job satisfaction and recognition.

The point is, how many of us are operating under false pretenses? How many of us are presuming we know what our employees want without asking?

Don't we stress the importance of finding out what the customers need before we decide which benefits to promote? Of course we do. Otherwise we run the risk of promoting the wrong benefits and losing the sale.

Isn't the same true with employees? Shouldn't we find out their real wants and needs and provide those?

While writing this book, I met with the director of a major international conglomerate. Their company had subsidiaries ranging from shoe polish to oil field supplies. They had gone from strength to strength in recent years.

He worked for headquarters and interfaced with the subsidiaries. I asked him the secret of their success. Without giving it much thought, he said, "Our financial package is the biggest incentive."

But I wasn't satisfied. I asked what really motivated his people, what gave them their job satisfaction. Gradually we started to dig deeper into the management style of the company.

We started to see that the nucleus of the company was composed of people who had worked together closely for many years; that they had worked in teams to bring subsidiaries up from failure through survival and finally growth; that their recognition of each other's capability extended into today's projects; and that the challenge of bringing more companies into profitable positions far outweighed their financial compensation.

RECOGNITION IS THE ANTIDOTE TO REJECTION

So, there it was again, recognition and job satisfaction at the top of the scale of importance! But, we ask ourselves, how do we recognize sales force needs? Aren't salespeople different from other employees?

The answer is yes. Salespeople are different. The difference is that they need even more recognition! Why? The answer is quite basic and logical.

Take a minute to think about recognition. The opposite of recognition is rejection. Every day salespeople are facing rejection. In fact, the proportion of rejection they face is higher than in any other job.

If they're doing their job right, they face rejection day in and day out. They face it when trying to close a sale, when trying to make an appointment, and at every stage of objection throughout the sales process.

RECHARGE THE BATTERY

Rejection is a draining process. It drains us of our enthusiasm, our confidence, our zest in life. Just as a battery that is drained needs recharging before it operates again, so do people. Recognition is the charge we need to overcome rejection.

Usually those people who don't deal in sales don't understand this. They find it annoying that salespeople require recognition. Sometimes this annoyance leads to pulling back from giving the salespeople what they really need, and this causes their motivation to suffer.

As managers, we need to make people aware of sales force needs, if we are to get the best results. We need everyone pulling together.

The next time you ponder ways to motivate the sales force, you can focus on ways to restore recognition, ways to recharge the battery. The results are immediate, as well as cost effective.

RECOGNITION OFFERS MANY OPTIONS

Recognition comes in many forms. It comes in listening to people--listening to their ideas, their problems, their goals, their needs. One-to-one communication can be the most powerful motivator in the world.

Do you realize how much the employee gains from the attention of the boss? A once-a-week, undivided ten minutes of face-to-face contact with the immediate boss does more for motivation than five dozen quick hellos.

In big companies, ten minutes with the chief executive will carry an employee through the year, or even through their career.

The exceptional Chief Executives I know give recognition to the employees for their specific performance. They relate it to the company's success as easily and sincerely as they do anything in life.

They've learned that a person's continued motivation is reliant upon the recognition of his or her efforts and contribution. Shouldn't we all take time to develop the same skill and understanding? Is this kind of recognition expensive? No.

Recognition comes in many forms, and they all bring cost effective results. It can be seeing one's name in print, a written or verbal announcement of competition winners, target achievers, and so on.

It can be verbal recognition of an individual or a group at a management meeting, a committee meeting or a council meeting.

One of the best group motivators I've known is Keith Barrett, who chaired the London Chamber of Commerce and Industry West Section before I became Chairman. He had exceptional ability to give positive reinforcement and recognition to the group for its actions.

His recognition was always to the point. Statements such as, "Due to your enormous support and hard work, we've now achieved such and such" kept each of us involved and working toward the committee's goals.

Shouldn't we all use specific recognition to ensure the highest contribution from our people? Shouldn't we take the advice of Jean Morgan-Bryant, who won the export award, and gave personal attention to everyone's needs?

What does each person in your team need? Each is different, and spending time with them is essential if we are to recognize their needs and motivate them to the best possible performance.

Remember to develop areas of improvement:

***Recharge the motivational battery
with recognition.***

ACTION SHEET
Chapter 18

Ideas for Development:

1. Acknowledge the fact that money is not always the top motivator.
2. If you want to raise personal performance levels, give people your personal attention. You're more powerful than you think.
3. Remember that needs are individualistic.
4. Recognize that recognition is the antidote to rejection.
5. Select the recognition form that fits the individual.
6. List other points here:
7.
8.

Of the above ideas, which one is likely to yield the best results?

What percentage of sales (or performance) increase could realistically be expected?

How long would it take: to develop the idea? to get results?

Who would have to be involved?

What date should we start?

What is the first step I should take?

What Business Are We Really In?

If the railroad barons in the United States had sat down 50 years ago and defined the business they were really in, the nature of their companies would be completely different. Their real business, of course, was not the railroad itself but transportation.

When air transportation arrived, they should have had the foresight to get involved in it, and not be left behind. They would have prevented their dramatic decline in sales.

Believe it or not, business, and even governments, often see their role differently than their customers see it. We have all seen government five-year plans that have been scrapped at the end of the first or second year. We have seen businesses with annual budgets set in January which rapidly change in March and change again in June because sales and expenditures don't meet their plan.

This level of uncertainty and change is often caused by inadequate analysis of customer needs. Do we really understand why our customers are dealing with us? Have we identified why we are unique and what special benefits we offer over our competition?

DON'T USE YESTERDAY AS TOMORROW'S GUIDELINE

Many managers assume they know what their business really is because they took over a successful product line. There appears to be growth and an improving market share and yet those products with an improving or commanding lead in competitiveness, are often the very ones that are about to become obsolete because of product lifecycles. The airplane was created long before it was realized that the railroads were a declining business.

Discovering what business we are really in can be answered only after hard thinking and studying. The right answer is usually anything but obvious.

FIND NEW APPLICATIONS

It's interesting to look at the business of Church and Dwight Company. They produce 'Pure Baking Soda' under the brand name of Arm and Hammer. The answer to their question, "What business are we in?" is indeed anything but obvious.

Their product is the most common and ordinary of products, pure bicarbonate of soda. However, the management team used an enlightened approach to broaden the business areas in which pure bicarbonate of soda competes. Not once, not twice, but at least five times!

In addition to their product acting as a leavening agent for the food industry when mixed with cream of tartar, it's also used medically for heartburn and the prevention of plaque on the teeth. Still farther afield is its use as a cleaning agent, a mild abrasive for the refrigerator, and yet again as a substance for absorbing food odors.

GO FOR DIVERSITY OF USERS

There you have five very diverse applications for the same product! One is human consumption, two applications are medical, two are cleaning related. Yet for all five its properties are identical. Can you diversify your application area? You may be surprised and your discovery can lead to new profits from new markets.

Sykes Consultants had a client with a similar opportunity. But the opportunity, like Arm and Hammer's, had to be discovered.

The company was faced with a product in the textile industry that was sadly and rapidly declining. It was being over-taken by man-made materials and cheaper imports. However, the fine natural qualities of the original product still attracted a loyal following, particularly users who had to comply with stringent fire regulations.

This application wasn't obvious to those who didn't look. A potentially huge new market has opened up for this company, utilizing their existing manufacturing technology and their channels of distribution.

INCREASE SALES ON MERIT, NOT CHANCE

This is a classic example of never accepting the obvious, never writing off the most basic of products. Ask yourself what consumers want that they haven't got. It is the ability to ask this question and to answer it correctly that usually makes the difference between a true growth company and one that depends on the rise of the economy for its development. Take the lead when looking for new applications for your product. Increase sales on your own merit, not on chance.

TEST THE WATERS CAREFULLY

How far afield should we go with applications? How quickly should we move?

Research shows that excellent companies stick to what they are best at, and only a move one manageable step at a time.

These companies keep to the business they know best and when entering new fields, they do it carefully. The best companies do not jump in too quickly. They test the waters carefully I first and if they don't have success, they withdraw quickly.

When we are challenging the nature of the business we are in, we should be careful that we are not too radical in moving into totally uncharted waters.

When we're looking for areas of improvement, we have to keep our eye on the customer. Find out what directions there needs are going. Remember the railroads. Remember the customers wanted transportation, but not necessarily train transportation. Focus on the fact that, with ingenuity, you can find new application areas for your products and services.

Remember to develop areas of improvement:

Look ahead to discover what direction your customer's needs are moving, in order to find new application areas for your products.

ACTION SHEET
Chapter 19

Ideas for Development:

1. Analyze what your customers gain from your product or service. This leads to perspective on opportunities and future product line investments.
2. Brainstorm new application areas for your current product.
3. Create diversity in your user base.
4. Ask yourself what consumers want what they haven't got.
5. Test the new application area carefully before entering fully.
6. List other points here:
7.
8.

Of the above ideas, which one is likely to yield the best results?

What percentage of sales (or performance) increase could realistically be expected?

How long would it take: to develop the idea? to get results?

Who would have to be involved?

What date should we start?

What is the first step I should take?

Chapter 20

What Separates Sales from Marketing?

It is absolutely fascinating that there is so much controversy over the difference between sales and marketing.

Invariably at the start of our sales seminars someone takes Bill or me aside and says, "I must get this issue cleared up. I'm embarrassed to ask, but what is the real difference between sales and marketing?"

The chart in Figure 1 shows the 'technical' differences. But first let's look at it from a common sense viewpoint. We don't really care what it's called, do we, as long as we get results from it. What we do want is to make sure that the component parts of each one is right and that the person running each is right.

Does each manager have the skills they need to handle the component parts? If you go to a seminar called 'Basics of Flying,' you don't want to find out it's being run by Oprah Winfrey, unless Oprah is a pilot. You might like to hear Oprah talk about interviewing, but for your purpose at that moment, you want to hear an expert on flying.

It's the same in sales and marketing. You don't want a good marketing person to be running sales or vice versa. There are many differing component parts in each.

All areas require different skills. The skills of your people are different as they themselves develop and as your personnel changes.

The important thing is to make sure that every part of the job is being carried out properly by people best able to handle that function. What fits your organization today may not be right tomorrow.

We live in a fast-changing world. We often find people being slaves to a structure that fits the organization and its people last year but not this year. All parts of the job must be carried out for a company to be successful, whether they fall under the marketing banner or the sales banner.

ADOPT A FLEXIBLE APPROACH

The companies with the best results take a flexible approach to the sales and marketing functions. As with work allocations on any project, organizational changes must be made to match the company's people resources.

Many companies undertake organizational changes as a matter of course. It can be rare for three to six months to pass without a major reshuffle in workload allocation. This happens normally as staff capability and company needs change.

The same is true of sales and marketing. It may seem logical to put a certain function under the heading of sales or the heading of marketing. But, if the available staff are not equipped to handle one function and can handle another function better, then a reshuffle shows wisdom.

If you want to move fast and improve returns, you have to look for the best people to handle the functions and be prepared to be flexible. You may run into resistance from people when a change is being contemplated, but that's one of the important roles of managers--the ability to handle objections and sell ideas in such a way that the employees see benefits to themselves and the company.

If your functions are not handled by the best people for the job, then you're not getting the best results. If you need to inspire change, you'll have to sell your ideas. As we said in earlier chapters, give them the facts and the benefits to let them *buy* your ideas. As every motivator knows, you are sure to get results when people support your ideas. To force issues without staff support is certain death. Even the best idea is sure to be undermined one way or another if you haven't *sold* the idea in terms of the benefits the people will gain.

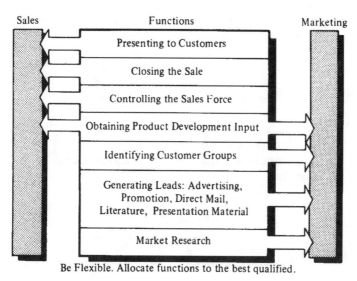

Be Flexible. Allocate functions to the best qualified.

Figure 1

MAKE SURE ALL FUNCTIONS ARE
CARRIED OUT BY THE BEST QUALIFIED PEOPLE

Regardless of how a company decides to allocate its sales and marketing functions, certain key responsibilities should be considered. Usually the responsibility for the functions are allocated as shown in Figure 1.

Within each function, the variety of tasks handled vary according to each company's needs. The important thing in achieving high results is to be sure that good, solid, airtight tracking systems are in place and that someone is held responsible for each function. Gray areas create chaos.

Tracking systems ensure that no inquiries are lost and that all sales practices are carried out on time.

CHOOSE THE HIERARCHY THAT SUITS YOUR NEEDS

An area of intense interest to companies is the hierarchy of the sales and marketing command. Should the sales side report to the marketing, or vice versa? Or should they both report to the company or division head?

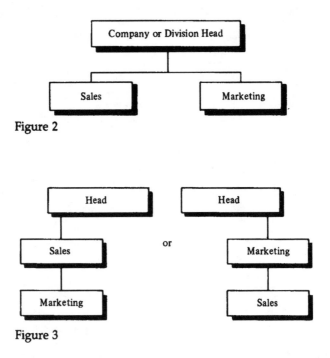

Figure 2

Figure 3

In companies where personalities, skills or views clash between sales and marketing, not an uncommon occurrence, the most workable solution is that shown in Figure 2. This can actually be healthy because strong ideas with different perspectives will go directly to the top for filtering.

The issue of whether sales should report to marketing or marketing to sales is determined by company preference (see Figure 3).

While the approach on the left side of Figure 3 is more traditional, we're finding that more large companies, especially in Europe, are moving toward the approach on the right. Their argument is that the marketing function provides more perspective, is more analytical by nature, and should have the overall responsibility. Our observation is that the decision is not based on rationale, but rather on who is at the top. More often than not, if the decision maker has a marketing background, marketing will reign. If that person's background is sales, sales will reign. So let's get away from party politics and on to results.

The important thing is to have 'the right people in the right place at the right time.' There are two ingredients to success:

1. Whoever reigns must understand both functions.
2. Whoever reigns must be a good motivator.

Without these two ingredients, the plan will fail. If the person who reigns over sales and marketing is a technocrat who does not understand the motivational needs of the sales force, the future can be grim. The best salespeople may go elsewhere. And, without a good sales force, sales go down. Bankruptcy looms.

CHANGE FUNCTIONAL RESPONSIBILITY AS YOUR NEEDS CHANGE

The next issue of interest, particularly in small and growing companies, is the question of adding sales and marketing people for the first time. How and when do we delegate these responsibilities away from the company head and bring in a new person? Should it be a sales function or a marketing function? The growth development in small companies usually looks like the diagram in Figure 4.

```
Company Head Includes
Sales and Marketing
in Own Responsibilities
```

Figure 4

In this initial stage, company heads usually handle sales and marketing functions themselves, along with other responsibilities. Although they may not feel they are large enough to treat sales and marketing as special functions, they nevertheless produce literature, sell the products or service, plan product development, and so on.

Figure 5

The next stage is to bring in one additional staff member to take part of the load off the company head (Figure 5). Usually we find that the new person handles sales, while the company head continues with marketing decisions related to advertising, promotion, exhibitions, and so on. But it doesn't have to be the case. The company head could hand over the marketing task and keep the sales responsibilities.

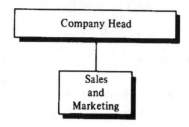

Figure 6

Later the company head may feel he or she needs to delegate more responsibility and may pass marketing over also, as shown in Figure 6.

With the right management controls in place, these moves usually stimulate growth because they allow the company head more time for planning and management.

Also, since the company head has controlled the function, he or she can quickly pinpoint areas of the job that are being handled well or need improvement. Therefore the changeover of responsibility is usually less dramatic and more effective than people anticipate. Many small companies delay this delegation step for fear of disruption and yet, when finally taking the leap, say that it was one of the most important steps in their development.

When we think about this dilemma, we see that the situation for small companies is similar to that of large companies. It's a matter of being flexible. It's recognizing the changing needs of the company and the capability of the people available.

A person who is too stretched for time is no different than a person without capability--the job won't be done effectively either way. Good managers have learned that surrounding themselves with good people brings rapid results, whether they run large or small companies.

Remember to develop areas of improvement:

Put people in charge of functions according to their abilities and the changing needs of the organization.

ACTION SHEET
Chapter 20

Ideas for Development:

1. Avoid being rigid about which functions are being handled by which department or person at the expense of getting results.
2. Delegate functions to the best qualified for each for that function.
3. Change who does what as your personnel and needs change.
4. Be flexible in your reporting structure making sure that whoever reigns over sales and marketing understands both functions.
5. Be sure whoever reigns is a good manager with motivational skills.
6. List other points here:
7.
8.

Of the above ideas, which one is likely to yield the best results?

What percentage of sales (or performance) increase could realistically be expected?

How long would it take: to develop the idea? to get results?

Who would have to be involved?

What date should we start?

What is the first step I should take?

Chapter 21

Management Controls: How to Make Them Effective

When my husband Tom and I lived in England one of our joys in life was taking our boat into the Thames River. Eventually it lead to the English Channel and the first thing we encountered near the coastline was a series of buoys floating in the water. These buoys stood up out of the water a few feet and had flashing colored lights on them.

Each buoy was a different color and we had to check the colors flashing on each one, then check our navigational chart, showing which color lights we should pass, to be sure we were going in the direction we intended to go.

It sounds easy, but it wasn't. The buoys were coming up fast, so by the time we checked the buoy on the right and the one on the left against the chart, we were on to the next set of buoys. The shoreline was getting further and further away and the feeling of being in deep water was literal.

MANAGEMENT CONTROLS KEEP YOU ON COURSE

We could see how easy it would be to go off course. If we didn't take corrective action immediately, we would be in big trouble. After two or three sets of wrong buoys, we knew it would be very difficult to get back on course. The weather could change and the current could be against us.

After passing three wrong buoys, getting on course again is more difficult than after one wrong buoy.

We don't go out to sea without charting our way ahead, and we don't set off and leave the chart behind. Because of the hazards at sea, we know every step of the way, whether we are on course or not. And when we go off course the first time, all hands are at the helm to help us back on course.

So it should be with management. *Controls systems link actual performance to the plan.* Isn't the direction we're going in business as important as the direction we're going at sea? Isn't it just as difficult to get back on course once we're off, as it is at sea?

Many companies think they can record results and compare them to their plan only every three months, or every year, or worse yet, never. 'We'll see where we'll go when we get out there.' A bit hazardous! In business, just as at sea, there are currents that work against us. The farther we let ourselves drift off course, the harder it will be to get back on when the currents come along. What if we don't take our plan with us?

If You Don't Know Where You're Going, You'll Probably End Up Somewhere Else according to the thought provoking book by Dr. Donald Campbell. If we don't have our plan with us to guide us every step of the way, we'll end up someplace else. That's expensive for business. And it's frustrating in life. We must have controls in business.

The best control is the ability to check actual sales performance against the plan on a regular, short-interval basis. Then, like the captain at sea, you can take quick corrective action when you start to go off course.

If the intervals are too long between performance checks against the plan, it's more difficult to get back on course. If this necessity for checking performance against the plan to have control is so self-evident, why aren't companies using management controls to get better results?

DON'T MISTAKE REPORTING SYSTEMS FOR CONTROL

The first reason is that they sometimes mistake a reporting system for management control. *A management control system MUST link actual performance to the plan.*

A system that records only the past performance without linking it to the company plans is not a control system. It's only a reporting system.

This is more common than you think. Bill and I have known company directors, both in our consulting and in the seminars, who say, "We have great management controls. We have performance reports coming off our computer as often as we want them. Yes, we have more than enough controls."

What they don't realize is that reports that measure results without comparing it to the target, are not controls. What good does it do you to know where you are if you don't know where you should be?

Therefore, controls aren't as good as they could be because the results aren't compared against the plan often enough. Then we also have to consider the plan itself.

When you're examining your plan, the question you need to ask yourself is, "Do we have our plan broken down into meaningful segments?"

The segmentation can be very useful in looking at each product group. If you look at the sales figures within product groups objectively, you see things that help you with your plan.

USE YOUR HISTORY TO SEGMENT YOUR PLAN

It's helpful to know about your past in order to look at the future objectively. If you're going to build an effective growth strategy, you need to know where your strengths have been and look for a trend for the future. You need to know *exactly* which product sectors you've had the most success in. You need to know *exactly* which customer sectors have been most important.

Your plan will only be as good as your precise knowledge of your company. I say precise because all of us have impressions of the past that prove to be less than accurate, when we look closely at actual data.

One client of ours had a lasting impression of an agent who performed well two years ago. His recent performance was dismal, yet the client clung optimistically to that agent long after hope was gone.

To avoid misimpressions, we must do an accurate analysis of sales by product and by customer sectors or industries.

Similarly, we might have a lasting impression of three big orders in one product category and lose sight of the fact that the small orders together are more important.

In order to be objective, we have to see actual facts, not just rely on hearsay, or on memory of past sales. If you don't see your situation accurately, your plan won't serve you as well as it could.

You might think that your gut feeling is right about sales breakdown by product and by customer or by territory but until you get it down on paper in black and white, it's meaningless. Trust me, it's true.

Most of us want to get on with the job and not take time out for meaningless analysis, but this is NOT the place to cut corners. If you take time to do the analysis, the results will be worth their weight in gold.

CHART YOUR HISTORY

I advocate putting statistics on sales breakdowns into chart form. A picture is worth a thousand words.

Here's what happened to a machinery company we worked with. They had figures that remained static for almost a five-year period. But the sales figures remained static only because of inflation. The actual number of products they were selling each year was going down. They quickly bundled together the numbers of units sold for each product group, and put the unit figures in bar graph form (Figure 1). This gave the directors a new, and truer, perspective.

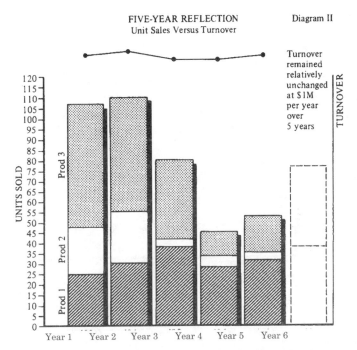

FIVE-YEAR REFLECTION
Unit Sales Versus Turnover

Diagram II

The bar graph shows quickly that product group 2 is looking hopeless, group 1 is holding its own, and group 3 is making a comeback. By looking at the number of units sold, rather than just the turnover, you now have accurate, indisputable facts about each product segment. You can see the trends. You can combine these trends with your knowledge of market demands to determine the plan for the future.

You can use segmentation not only to understand each product group as the company above did, but also to understand each customer group.

One client did this successfully. They were a very prestigious company in the marine engineering industry. They designed nozzles for ship propellers that improve fuel efficiency, velocity, and maneuverability. The nozzles were used on everything from naval ships and tugs to small fishing boats.

We encouraged the company directors to break down their sales history into finer detail than was available on their day-today management report in order to develop a plan for the future.

They divided their sales statistics into product sectors and then into territory sectors (Figure 2). They put it into an easily digestible graph. One look at the graph gave them more insight than written figures. They could easily see that the fishing sector produced a high volume of orders. They were now in a position to ask themselves questions about where to take their company in the future. The fishing sector produced more unit sales but the naval sector produced higher value sales.

PAST SALES ANALYSIS HELPS YOU PLAN THE FUTURE
By Industry, By Area

	Naval	Tug	Oil Rig Supply Vessel	Fishing	Drilling	Bulk Carrier	Ferries	Workboat
USA Sector A	★★★★★★★ ★★★	★★★★★ ★		★★★★★★ ★★★★★★ ★★★★★★	★	★★★		
USA Sector B		★★★★★ ★★		★★★★★ ★★★★★ ★★★★★				★★★★★ ★★★★★ ★★
USA Sector C		★★		★★★★★★ ★★★★★★ ★★★★				
UK		★★		★★★	★			
Canada				★★★★★				
Egypt		★					★★★★★ ★★	
Norway		★★★	★★★	★	★			
Iceland								
Singapore		★★★★	★★★					
Holland		★★	★					

Figure 2

What if they hadn't produced the graph, but only saw the sales figures on paper? They, like owners of most companies, would only know the total sales value. They wouldn't know how many units were sold to shipping and naval. They wouldn't know which countries each were sold to.

MAKE YOUR PLAN,
THEN COMPARE YOUR RESULTS DAILY

Doesn't segmenting make sense? Use it for planning the future after you've analyzed the past.

In our *Develop Effective Sales* seminars, Bill and I have members focus on specific areas of past performance, then plan the future.

By doing this, they can accurately see their strengths and know more about what customers have really wanted from them. Only then can they plan their future. And only by having a segmented plan can they have management controls.

Here's an example. One seminar attendee, Bob Williams, had a plan for a 20% growth for his company in the next year. We encouraged him to divide his growth targets into specific segments.

So he said, "OK, we'll increase our sales to our current customers by 10%, and get the other 10% from completely new customers."

"And when will your reps have time to visit the new prospects?"

"Oh, they'll just fit that in," he said.

"Well, let's see," I said, "let's just see how many appointments they need to do. And don't forget the calls to make the appointments as well. Let's do a specific analysis, and see how much work it amounts to for each rep each day. Then, when you know *exactly* what's required, you can *monitor* and *control* it."

We were going gently with Bob, but we knew that if he didn't have an exact plan, he wouldn't know when he was going off course. If he didn't know exactly what activity was needed day by day, by each person, he wouldn't know if his growth was on target. He would be letting it go to chance until the end of the month or the end of the year.

"OK, Bob, let's start from the top. We'll flip chart it." It looked like this:

Growth Plan
Segmented for Management Control Purposes

Goal: 20% Sales Growth Wanted

How: 10% from New, 10% from Old Customers

Breakdown of Total Workload:

Business from New Customers:
- ✓ 10% growth will mean we need 100 new customers. We will have to see 10 prospects in order to gain one new customer. Therefore 1OOO prospects need to be seen.
- ✓ Each prospect will require approximately five telephone calls before an appointment can be arranged. Therefore 5000 phone calls need to be made.
- ✓ (Add here any other workload requirements such as mail shots or direct mail to be sent, etc.)

Business from Old Customers:
- ✓ Growth of 10% will mean we need new business from 100 old customers.
- ✓ We will have to see three old customers in order to gain business from one.
- ✓ Therefore 300 old customers need to be seen.
- ✓ Each old customer will need approximately two telephone calls before an appointment can be arranged. Therefore 600 phone calls need to be made.

Total:
- ✓ 1300 customers need to be seen (1000 new and 300 old) 5600 phone calls need to be made to make appointments. (5000 to new and 600 to old customers)

Breakdown of Daily Workload for Growth:
- ✓ We have 50 weeks (52 minus 2 for vacations, etc.)
- ✓ This breaks down to 20 new prospects each week (1000 divided by 50 weeks). And six old customers each week (300 divided by 50 weeks).

✓ We have five days per week.
✓ This breaks down to four new prospects each day (20 divided by five days), and one to two old customers each day (six divided by five days).

Divide this by the number of salespeople you have, and you have the true daily workload for appointments, in addition to your current workload.

But we're not finished yet. Repeat the process for the number of telephone calls that need to be made daily, per person.

REALLOCATE WORK

If the results astound you, look again. You may want to reallocate work to other members of staff or create other solutions. It's better to find out now and monitor and control it throughout the year, then to ignore the workload and find out too late that your targets are not going to be met.

The same system works for small companies.

A woman I know in network marketing, wanted to establish distributors to sell health products. Her plan was to distribute leaflets to entice would-be distributors for evening demonstrations. We did a mini-version of the above analysis.

She quickly saw that the number of distributors she wanted would require many times more leaflets and demonstrations than were possible, so she changed her strategy to include advertising and other methods. But without doing the analysis, she told me, she would have wasted six months of effort and caused tremendous demotivation.

DON'T BE COMPLACENT

This is a typical shortcoming of small and large companies, so don't be complacent. Create a daily monitoring and control system for yourself which compares actual to your plan.

In my book *Secrets of the World's Top Sales Performers*, I featured the strategy of a top salesperson who was untouchable. Year after year he was the company's top achiever – worldwide! He told me repeatedly, "Christine anybody can do it, anybody can do it."

Here's what he did. He calculated that he needed to sell five products every day to stay at the top. So each morning he loaded five products into his car, and he didn't quit until he was finished. If for some reason he only sold four on Monday, he disciplined himself to sell six on Tuesday. In that way he kept his 'five per day' average up to date, and didn't slip behind. He shared his secrets with all who cared to hear. But only he made the ranks of top sales performers of the world. Isn't it worth considering for yourself?

If your people need to make 10 telephone calls per day to make prospect appointments, make sure it's done.

If they make NO calls on Monday, they'll have 20 on Tuesday. If they skip Monday and Tuesday, they have 30 to make on Wednesday. You see the point. If you want real results, create wall charts and record actual against target, not just on sales, but on appointments, phone calls, and everything else. Don't make it a punishment system. Instead make it an acknowledgement system!

You see the problem. Most people try to fit it in. They work without a monitor and control formula.

On the above basis, if you let your new customer acquisition go until the end of the month, you'll have 200 phone calls to do. That's why most sales targets are not met. People don't segment them into daily tasks.

Use specifics in developing your plan and in measuring the results against the plan each step of the way. Keep your plan with you and compare your results to the plan every step of the way.

Remember to develop areas of improvement:

**Segment your plan and your results,
then compare, compare, compare.**

ACTION SHEET
Chapter 21

Ideas for Development:

1. Remember that management control systems keep you on course and provide early alert to going off course. They are worth every minute of time and effort to create and implement.
2. Don't mistake reporting systems for control systems. The latter COMPARES *actual* results to *targets*.
3. Chart the history of your product sales by number of products sold per product group, not just dollar value sold.
4. Chart the history of your product sales to each customer sector or industry group, by number of products sold, not just dollar value sold.
5. THEN make a detailed target for each product and industry sector. Calculate the activity needed to produce it.
6. Then monitor and control results against target, not only in sales, but in the activities needed to produce the sales.
7. List other points here:
8.

Of the above ideas, which one is likely to yield the best results?
What percentage of sales (or performance) increase could realistically be expected?
How long would it take: to develop the idea? to get results?
Who would have to be involved?
What date should we start?
What is the first step I should take?

PART 7

SUCCESSES AND FAILURES

...IN OVERSEAS MARKETS

Chapter 22

How to Plan Your Entry for Maximum Results

Yes, selling into foreign markets can be extremely lucrative. Some companies even sell exclusively to export markets. If they can sell all of their goods abroad, it stands to reason that most of us can sell some of our goods abroad.

The question is how to enter as profitably as possible, with as few mistakes as possible. And competition is growing. As of this writing, the State of California alone placed fifth in world trade, taking over that position from the UK. Think of the potential there is for other American companies to start exporting!

WASTE NO TIME

There's no time to waste. Competition is increasing. If we don't learn to meet the competitors head on in overseas markets, we'll be facing them in our own markets as they start to import.

Two companies were recently featured on television. Both made the same product. One had outdated production and management techniques. It was losing ground rapidly to the Korean imports. The other company had developed high productivity by investing in machinery and by putting management controls and incentives into place. They were selling successfully *against* the Koreans on the Koreans' home ground with the identical product!

The first company complained that, "Our problem is lack of government intervention. We want protection against imports." The second company knew that reliance on government policy was not the solution. They took responsibility for their own future and planned a success strategy that would work--with or without government intervention.

Regardless of what we believe about protection from imports, the fact is that we can not predict government policy. If we are to profit, we have to develop our own ways to succeed.

Whether we export or not, we need to understand foreign products and marketing. We'll be faced with these, here and abroad. The sooner we grasp the differences, the sooner we'll succeed.

Getting into foreign markets profitably is a three-step process. *One is the plan, two is the implementation, three is the follow-up.* Where many companies go wrong is with the plan; then the implementation and follow-up are worthless. It becomes an exercise of throwing good money after bad.

The answer is to look at all the alternatives for entering the market. Will you sell direct, work through a distributor, or perhaps sell your technology? Only after considering your alternatives, can you can decide which is most lucrative as part of your planning process.

FIRST, PLAN CAREFULLY, CONSIDERING ALL OPTIONS

One company came to us and asked us to find and appoint distributors for them in overseas markets. They had already rejected setting up their own premises. They thought that selling through distributors was the only alternative. But the exchange rate had turned against them.

After investigating the market, we were attracted to another option. What if they were to have heir product manufactured abroad under license? By licensing they could sell their technology and in return get a front-end fee and royalties. They stood to gain more that way than they would by direct sales.

They would derive three benefits. First, they would have a yearly income from royalties with an agreed minimum guarantee. Second, they would have less management and staff involvement, meaning that they could use their time for other expansion activities. And third, they would not have to finance any expansion of their manufacturing facility. That is certainly a lucrative alternative to consider.

EXPLORE PROFITABLE ALTERNATIVES

Look at your alternatives in depth. Don't have blinder vision, don't restrict your opportunities to what works in other places. A foreign market is indeed foreign. The culture is different and so are the opportunities.

When you're planning your market entry, be sure to look at all alternatives. It takes a little more time and a little more ingenuity, but the results pay off.

The opportunity to 'license' was often thought of as relating to developing countries. But that's not the case. It works well between or within any set of countries because the buyers may find it cheaper to purchase your expertise than to develop their own. For you, the seller, a know-how fee plus ongoing royalties may prove to be more profitable than selling the product direct.

A large investment bank we worked with wanted to fund a textile factory that would produce $13,000,000 worth of clothing each year. They could have drawn upon local expertise to set up the factory and the product line, but they didn't.

They knew from previous experience that buying the know-how for the production and product line would save time. Because of buying the technology, several of their previous factory start-ups showed profits within one year of incorporation. We worked with them to find a licenser.

WHAT'S RIGHT FOR YOU?

The point is, you need to choose the method that is right for you and the best option in the country being considered. Don't go for convenience. Cutting the plan short will lead to disaster in the implementation and follow-up stages. You'll spend time and money trying to make something out of nothing.

A common error companies make is to appoint agents they meet during an exhibition or tradeshow. They may seem right at the time, but further investigation proves they don't have the right sales contacts, service capability, and so on. A trip to the country saves you from throwing good money after bad.

What's right for your competitors or right for you five years from now may not be right today. When it comes to acquisitions, joint ventures, and setting up premises, you need to proceed with caution. Be sure you know the culture and the marketplace.

Bill tells the story of two different companies--one company American and one British--trying to get into each other's markets.

The British company bought out an American company and afterwards discovered that the salaries of the American staff members were much higher than those of the British counterparts. So they reduced the salaries of the American executives, and then wondered why they weren't content to stay! They thought the Americans would stay because the bigger parent company would offer more career opportunities. They were wrong. They found themselves trying to run a new company in a country they knew nothing about, with no experienced executives!

In the other story, an American company was new to foreign marketing and decided incorrectly that they would set up premises in Europe. They would have one location in England to serve Norway, France, Sweden, and England, with no local support in the other three countries. Their idea that they could sell direct, without agents and without people who spoke the language and knew the culture, brought them disastrous results. Had they examined their options, such as appointing local agents and distributors, they would have achieved better results.

Although both companies did well in their own markets, they failed to choose the right options when their companies entered overseas markets.

Options like licensing look complicated to some companies on the surface, but when they dig deeper into it, they see it can be less complicated than taking an obvious route like the two companies above. All options should be considered if you want to maximize your success.

Don't take what looks like an easy route and then find out, halfway down the road, that it's the wrong choice.

SECOND, IMPLEMENT THE PLAN, GOING AROUND THE ROADBLOCKS

When you're getting into a market, put your best foot forward. Present yourself properly. Don't send the wrong person or the wrong literature. Don't go unprepared. Believe it or not, we've seen heads of companies go abroad with no literature, no photographs, no samples – even no business cards! They're too pressed for time and so unprepared that they throw away their opportunity.

If you don't know the market, don't try to make decisions without local expertise. Dealing in foreign markets is like working your way through a maze in the shortest possible time. To get guidance through the maze, you would choose an expert to show you through--someone with proven ability, not a man on the street who's never been through it before.

USE LOCAL CONSULTANTS FOR CREATIVE SOLUTIONS

At the implementation stage, you'll find obstacles. You need people who can overcome the obstacles.

We had a client company in textile supplies wanting to sell into a developing country. But their product was on the restricted list. So they thought they would have to set up a local operation to either produce or package the product there. But our consultant, who knew the governmental decision-making process, had more insight. He was able to link the company up with a local manufacturer who could import the product because he had the authority to veto import restrictions on his product group. This manufacturer was able to sell his own product and our client's product through his already established network. The problem was solved quickly and profitably. Without the local consultant, the picture would have been different..

Another company, one in pharmaceuticals, wanted to export to a Middle East country. They heard that committee approval of their product was required. This would supposedly take two years. We shortened the cycle to two months instead of two years by having consultants assist.

Here's what we did. Prominent doctors in the country were visited by our consultant and told about the product. Then we sent government committee members carefully prepared information packages with all the material needed for approval. This included product data sheets, packaging, and so on. Before the committee was due to meet, we asked if our client company could send a representative to attend the meetings.

The committee received the representative and listened to his presentation. They were delighted that the company cared enough to show such interest. The approval cycle then took its normal channel with one exception. The consultancy intervention moved the file from the bottom to the top of the pile for consideration. It not only assured consideration, it cut a two year waiting list.

USE DETERMINATION TO OVERCOME ROADBLOCKS

Use determination as we did with this company. Even on the smallest issue, when encountering roadblocks, look for alternatives.

Don't give up. Otherwise little obstacles lead to bigger ones. Remember the textile company that overcame import restrictions. Remember the pharmaceutical company that overcame the two-year wait on committee approval. If there's a will, there's a way. Keeping your sales growth target in mind helps to increase your determination.

If you know the market potential--if you know what results you're aiming for--your priority will remain high. So will the company commitment to the project. This will carry you through the difficult times and keep you from abandoning the effort midstream.

THIRD, FOLLOW IT UP
AS IF IT WAS YOUR ONLY MARKET

This is the most common and the most heartbreaking of all reasons for failure. After thousands of dollars are spent on a trip abroad and after endless hours of preparation, the executive arrives home to a full desk of paperwork.

Unfortunately, the follow-up that needs to be done on the foreign market often loses out to other pressures. You can understand that the people overseas, not receiving the appropriate follow-up, presume interest has died. Then their interest and enthusiasm start to fade. If you want to succeed in starting up a foreign market, you might try mentally treating it as your only market. Give it the attention it deserves.

"Out of sight, out of mind" applies to exporting more than most other things. No matter what country you're dealing in, give it continuous attention.

Having local support of some kind has always proved to increase sales. Regardless of your industry or the country, you can engage local people cost effectively to keep things moving, to alert you to problems, and to save you trips to the marketplace. The extra effort pays valuable dividends. There are many consultants like ourselves and others who can help you to motivate agents and keep your project alive.

REMEMBER THE HUMAN FACTOR

Don't forget the human factor when you're dealing overseas. People in some countries expect to get to know you and need to be entertained. In other countries a straightforward, direct approach is the only way to succeed.

Whether you're choosing an agent or acquiring a company, the human factor is critical. Whoever you're sending abroad to follow up on business needs to be the type who can adapt to each situation. The dynamic sales and marketing director of a large company might be perfect for large-scale negotiations. Yet someone else could be more effective in smaller developing countries. Yet another personality could be needed to interface with entrepreneurs during acquisition discussions. Put the right person on the right job.

The points we've discussed here are sensible, workable principles. But as Samuel Coleridge said, "Common sense in an uncommon degree is what the world calls wisdom." Foreign marketing requires greater wisdom because of the greater parameters involved. If you want to add markets profitably, we suggest you get a start, work aggressively, and follow up closely. And more than every other factor, don't neglect making the right plan, the rest is fruitless.

Remember to succeed in overseas markets:

Consider all options,
then give it undying determination

ACTION SHEET
Chapter 22

Ideas for Development:

1. Think about all your alternatives such as selling direct, selling through agents and distributors, setting up premises or selling your technology so that your product is manufactured abroad under license.
2. When appointing an agent, do a thorough search and resist the temptation to appoint people you've met at trade shows. Convenience now will be costly later.
3. Don't assume that salaries and practices are the same abroad as they are at home. Research everything.
4. Use local consultants to help you through the maze and find angles for profitable market entry.
5. Follow up quickly with needed and promised actions.
6. List other points here:
7.
8.

Of the above ideas, which one is likely to yield the best results?

What percentage of sales (or performance) increase could realistically be expected?

How long would it take: to develop the idea? to get results?

Who would have to be involved?

What date should we start?

What is the first step I should take?

Chapter 23

Finding the Right Agent or Distributor: It's Like Finding a Needle in the Haystack

See what errors you can spot as you read the following scenario. Look for time delays, expenditure and lackadaisical approach.

HOW NOT TO PROCEED

January—Month 1

In January, Colin Jones, who heads up his own company making food processing equipment, decided to export to England. He told his sales director, John Martin, to stop there on his way back from another overseas trip to get a feel for the competition. He did that in May. After three days looking around the market at competitive equipment and prices, he wrote up his findings and told Colin Jones that he felt there was a market for them.

May--Month 5

Colin and John were happy that the market looked promising. Their next job was to find an agent. They remembered an agent who approached them at an exhibition last year, and so in July they wrote to him to see if he would be willing to represent them. The agent wrote back with a positive response in early September, so Colin and John flew over in October for discussions.

October--Month 10

They came home feeling optimistic. They hadn't agreed on an agency contract in writing because the agent wanted to do a market survey, and John and Colin needed to finalize their own prices, including delivery.

Four months passed and they heard nothing from the agent. Finally, contacting him by telephone, they found out that he was no longer interested. That occurred in February.

March--Month 15

By March, 15 months after their decision to break into the market, they decided to broaden their net and examine several other agents before leaping at another one. However, in April they received a cable from a small contracting company referred by the first agent. This company said they could acquire orders quickly and asked for several quotations. John and Colin thought they had better have a firsthand look at the company and its customers, but to save costs, only Bill flew over this time. They realized that he could easily handle it on his own.

June--Month 17

Things looked promising, and they sent their first shipment over at cost to break into the market in June. The first new customers were acquired, the market was buoyant, and Colin made preparations to increase his production capacity. That was in June.

December--Month 24

By December the story was different. They weren't hearing from the agent any more. Orders had stopped. Colin managed to find out that the company had changed into a different area of business and had not been servicing their products properly. That wouldn't help their reputation. They sat back reflecting on the time, energy, and money spent, and wondered where they had gone wrong.

Summary:
- 24 months elapsed.
- Three plane tickets.
- Travel expenses.
- 15 working days of managerial time away from home base.
- High managerial planning time.
- Shipment at cost.
- No progress on market entry.

That's the experience of Colin Jones and John Martin. The story is strikingly like those we hear from companies day in and day out.

WHAT WENT WRONG?

Why is it that Colin and John didn't have more structure in their method of finding a good agent? Perhaps it's the lack of seeing their incentive clearly. If they had determined that the market could account for a certain percentage growth in their company in 12 months, and had they set stage by stage sales targets, would they have perhaps not let so much time pass between communications?

Alsc, had their incentive been clear and their targets set, wouldn't they have put more effort into looking at several agents and not simply gamble on the first person they thought of, the one they met at a trade stand? Maybe, maybe not.

Let's compare selecting an agent to hiring sales personnel. I'm always amazed that companies spend so much time and effort recruiting salespeople for their home base, and so little time and effort recruiting overseas agents. Yet an overseas agent can do more to increase turnover by opening up the market of a whole country than a salesperson can do at home in a single territory.

When companies hire salespeople, they train them. They put together targets. They watch over them. Yet when they take on agents, their attitude is less committed. Then they ask why they don't get commitment back!

USE A STRUCTURED APPROACH

If you want to find the right agent you need to use a structured approach. You can't gamble. You don't appoint agents you pick up at an exhibition without checking their references any more than you would pick up hitchhikers along the road and appoint them as your sales reps at home base. The gamble may pay off once but, let's face it, the odds are against you.

How many agents do you need? The U.S. market, for example, is said to have 10 times the buying power of the U.K. That means that it's worth 10 countries the size of Britain. Yet many overseas companies see the U.S. as a single market and give it comparatively little attention.

Several American companies we know have the same problem with Europe. It seems far away and it's easy to think of it as one place. If you appoint an agent for all of Europe, you'll find that the language, cultural differences and distances make it difficult to sell across borders.

The way we advise companies to find agents is to use a structured approach. Just as in the last chapter, you want to examine your options.

This time the options relate to representation. Will your agent be an importer, a distributor, another manufacturer who will act as an agent, or what? Ask yourself, "Who do they sell to now? What targets will they and we aim for together? What training will we give? How often will we see them?

All these things are important in finding the right agent. Use a structured approach, don't gamble. It's better to find out differences of opinion before the relationship begins than later. Will all or part of that person's time be allocated? How much time? Will the head of the company promote your product or will one of the junior staff? Will you divide the advertising budget between yourselves? How much? When and where will it be spent?

Perhaps it sounds like too much trouble. But successful companies operate this way. They treat export with as much care, or more, than their own market. And why not? The return can be proportionally greater!

HOW TO PROCEED

Here's a company that did it right. You'll see a striking difference in its planning, its timing, and its management practices to the one above.

At the same time that Colin Jones decided to export to England, so did Andy Smith. Andy's company made similar equipment and was located near Colin's.

January--Month 1

The month was January. Andy knew from his research that his products could meet England's requirements. If he could gain only 3% of the market he could reach his growth objective. He called in his sales director, Mike Northfield, to make a plan with deadlines for each stage. They listed their goals as:

- Structured market entry
- Effective use of management time
- Ambitious increase in revenue--25% in 12 months
- Steady, controlled growth--100% in three years

Andy emphasized to Mike that he wanted every avenue of representation to be explored before deciding what type of agent to choose. He wanted Mike to look for companies with:

- Well established sales contacts in their field.
- Good reputation with users and suppliers.
- Technical and service capability.

These companies could be any of the following three:

- Agents or importers
- Distributors
- Compatible manufacturers who could act as agents

Mike went back to his desk and thought about every way he could use to identify companies in these three categories. He made a list of all the trade associations, government departments, end users, and his personal contacts who might be able to help him.

By the third week in January he had sent letters to these people asking for their recommendations on companies they felt were qualified to act as agents--such as importers, distributors, and compatible manufacturers.

February--Month 2

By February he had learned of many companies in the three categories. He contacted the heads of those companies by letter, stressing the benefits and features of his products. He listed his sales objectives and suggested ways his company could support their sales efforts if they became agents. He asked them to respond before the first of March with details of their company.

He took special effort to follow up each letter three days after the letter arrived with a phone call to prove his seriousness and to further entice the company. His second reason for calling was that he was able to glean his own impressions of the company from his calls: the way the phone was answered, the way messages were taken, the way his questions were answered. He knew this was the way his future customers would be handled too.

April--Month 4

He listed the companies in priority order by what he had heard about them and from them. In April, after confirming his plan with Andy, he contacted the top six companies on his list to arrange to visit them from May 17 to 20.

May--Month 5

Before flying over, he and Andy made pricing decisions and on how long they could hold the prices considering exchange rate fluctuations. If they obtained orders they would buy currency forward, and so they included these costs in their pricing policy.

They also included shipping door-to-door to make buying easy for the customer. Mike made up price lists in U.K. sterling amounts, because he knew people preferred to deal in their own currency. Also, he knew that having the converted price lists with him would help him to keep his mind on the people and the negotiations instead of the calculator.

He arranged his visits so as to see the *least* likely company first. This would help him to become familiar with the industry and the way it operates in the U.K. This would give him preparation for going into meetings with the most likely candidates. It would also allow him to practice his own presentation and to see how to refine his package to meet the overseas needs. He remembered that the British are less direct in their approach so he carefully planned to make his benefits and targets come across gradually in his discussions.

The meetings went well and on the third day he came to a full working agreement with one of the companies to import his product, and later to manufacture it under license if the sales targets were reached. The manufacturing option would also protect Andy and Mike if the exchange rate went against them.

Mike made a second visit the following day to iron out the first order details, the sales targets, the training, literature, and the dates that each would carry out the actions. They put their joint commitments on paper.

The head of the company told Mike he was impressed with his efficiency. He said he liked to deal with companies who were organized from the beginning because they always performed better later.

Then he told Mike of another foreign supplier he'd dealt with in the past who didn't keep to his commitments. He didn't want to get burned twice. There was a lot of work involved in securing orders and it was a disappointment to have suppliers let you down. He had almost refused to see Mike, in fact, but Mike's efficiency and persistence throughout had told him to take a second chance. Now he was glad he had. He was sure their working relationship would be mutually profitable.

On the fourth evening Mike boarded the plane to go home with an agency agreement in his pocket and satisfaction that his preparation had paid off. In addition he had an order worth 15% of his first year's target. But the order wasn't the end of the road. He knew Andy wanted steady, controlled growth and he knew he had found the right company to support their efforts for their three-year, 100% growth plan.

It had been an exhausting trip. It was a tempting thought to put all the paperwork away during the flight and catch a little sleep, but he knew his desk would be piled up with new demands on his first day back. He knew he'd better write his follow-up report, letters, plan of action, and commitments now while his notes were fresh in his mind.

He remembered hearing that the mind forgets 80% of what it hears after two days. Even though he had clear notes, he decided he'd better do it now while details were fresh in his mind. Then his follow-up points could be begun on his first day back. That would move them closer to the 100% growth plan.

As his plane approached home, he reflected on what a good feeling it was to work for a company that set specific growth plans. "When you make a contribution here, you know exactly how it fits into the total plan," he thought to himself. He knew Andy would be ecstatic with his results and give him recognition for his achievement.

Summary:
- 5 months elapsed.
- 1 plane ticket.
- travel expenses.
- 4 working days of management time away from home base.
- Effective managerial planning time.
- Shipment with profit.
- Progress on market entry (order worth 15% of first year's growth target).

That's the experience of Andy Smith and Mike Northfield.

During this session of our *Develop Effective Sales* seminars, we sometimes have people say they wish they had a Mike Northfield working for them. Others say they wish they had an Andy Smith as a boss! These kinds of people do exist. We know them and work with them.

Fumi Nakagome in Japan is a case in point. She knows how important the personal contact is to getting business. Her philosophy is, "Never write when you can call, and never call when you can visit." She should know, she's been a company President in Tokyo and has worked under three prime ministers in Japan as adviser on various issues.

If we want to find the right agent, we have to get out there and look. We have to visit agents and be sure we're making the right decision.

Finding the right agent is like finding a needle in the haystack, not because they don't exist, but because companies don't know how to look for them. They gamble on the first one that comes along rather than using a structured approach, as Mike Northfield did. They take the easy road, only to find out later that they've wasted their time, money, and effort.

Doing business successfully in an environment of uncertainty is almost impossible. Get advice from others who have succeeded. Bob Northfield didn't jump on a plane the minute Andy mentioned England. He contacted everyone he thought of who could help. He did it quickly and effectively.

All the planning and preparation you can do ahead will pay off. This is true of each and every country. Remember the two years wasted by Colin Jones and Bill Martin. Don't let it happen to you.

Remember to succeed in overseas markets:

Use a structured approach; don't gamble.

ACTION SHEET
Chapter 23

Ideas for Development:

1. Calculate prices in foreign currency and consider options for holding prices despite currency fluctuation.
2. Research your product's adaptability to the market place.
3. Research the market potential and competitors products.
4. Use a structured approach of setting targets, researching entry options, getting referrals, and contacting companies before your visit.
5. Visit at least three, choose one and set targets and follow up activities.
6. List other points here:
7.
8.

Of the above ideas, which one is likely to yield the best results?

What percentage of sales (or performance) increase could realistically be expected?

How long would it take: to develop the idea? to get results?

Who would have to be involved?

What date should we start?

What is the first step I should take?

Chapter 24

Wake up to Cultural Pitfalls
In Presentations, In Negotiations,
In Follow-Up

Some years ago on one of my trips to Egypt, I was in the procurement offices of the Egyptian National Railroad. I had an appointment with the director of the department, and when I went into the office, as so often happens in Egypt, there were several meetings going on at the same time in the same room. Over on one side of this very large room were four young Japanese gentlemen, with blueprints spread all over the table. They were casually dressed, well entrenched in their conversation, and clearly planning to stay for some time.

I returned the next day to see the director again and they were still there. I had the impression that they planned to stay for days or weeks.

I forgot about the situation until some trips later when I heard talk of the new high speed train to Alexandria. A friend advised me to take it because it was quicker than flying or driving--and the latest thing in Cairo. Everyone was talking about it.

When I arrived at the platform, the new train pulled in, and spread all across the side was a beautiful Japanese symbol. Yes, of course, it clicked. I'd forgotten--the Japanese had won that contract; they had stayed and negotiated as long as it took to win.

UNDERSTAND THE COMPETITOR'S BUSINESS STYLE

When we're dealing in foreign markets, we must remember that the competition can be fierce. We have many cultural differences to be aware of--not just the customer, but also the competitor.

I know another Japanese salesman who was sent to the Middle East to win a contract. He'd been there eight months and went back and forth to England occasionally for a short break. But he won't go home to Japan until he wins.

Yet how many of us would be prepared to stay abroad until we won?

The day is gone when we can insulate ourselves from the outside world. I can get to Japan, a third of the way around the world, in less time than it took my grandparents to travel by horse and buggy from Prague to their home in an outlying village. The world is closing in on us. Cultural understand are much more important now, if we are to win in international expansion.

UNDERSTAND THE CUSTOMER'S BUSINESS STYLE

If we step over the threshold into a new marketplace, the cultural differences are up to us to overcome. We have to play according to their rules.

That reminds me of a comment made by a foreign venture capitalist who acquired several private American companies. The advice he has for companies serious about acquisitions is to send someone from the parent company to negotiations who understands entrepreneurs. Doesn't that make sense for every business venture? Send someone who understands the players. Otherwise you lose the game. It's important in presentation, in negotiations, and in follow-up.

I remember one client who went to the Middle East without understanding the importance of building a social rapport with customers and agents. He had a difficult product line, one that was very price conscious, and our job of finding him an agent, was not an easy one.

During an interview, one agent casually invited everyone to lunch. The client refused the invitation. Naturally the agent was insulted.

Little did our client know that his chances of getting local representation were going down by the minute. Luckily our overseas consultant, who accompanied him saved the day by unobtrusively taking the client aside, explaining the situation, and turning the lunch decision around.

There you have it: A difficult product in a difficult market. You manage to find an agent, which is like finding a needle in a haystack, and the whole market is almost lost at the negotiation stage by a lack of cultural understanding.

One of America's biggest defense contractors recently sent a marketing executive over from the head office to present their case to the European ministries. This person had never before set foot outside American soil. His management style took no account of European habits. They perceived him as arrogant and aggressive. He hadn't taken the time to consult others to find out who the key players were, or find out about their needs and personalities.

After half a day of meetings, the British showed him the door, so he flew across the channel to upset the French.

Did he win either contract? No. Were the contracts important to the company? Yes. Did the marketing executive do his homework first by contacting his firm's overseas employees first to get their advice or their input? No. Why not? You tell us. Perhaps it was pride, perhaps politics, perhaps ignorance.

It's *people* who make or break business, *not necessarily* the product or the price. We see it every day. Companies spend hours, days, weeks, and months reducing their prices and talking about better products development. Then they send the wrong person or an untrained person over to the marketplace to represent them. The sale is lost the minute that person steps off the airplane.

Adapt Your Methods To Suit The Culture

Figure 1 shows the pitfalls most often seen in overseas selling. The four categories represent four segments of the sales process: preparation, presentation, negotiation, and follow-up.

Of all the segments, presentation and follow-up are the two in which most companies fall down when trying to do business in a foreign culture. Let's look at each segment to find ways of overcoming the pitfalls.

Pitfall A -- Preparation

The company fails to choose the right country for their product, or the right agent or entry mode.

Don't pick a country or agent for reason of ease rather than investigation. Be sure your product is right for the market, know if the market size is large enough to warrant your effort, speak the language, be sure you can service the marketplace, learn about cultural differences, and be sure your people can adapt.

Pitfall B -- Presentation

The content or style of the presentation is wrong for the marketplace.

Don't fail to adapt your presentation to local demands and customs. Remember the American who lost the European contracts. Make sure that your presentation material meets local standards, that the person doing the presentation will be accepted, that your pace of aggressiveness is right for the market, that you tell the benefits and features that are important locally.

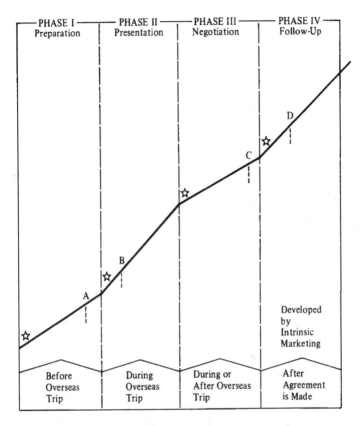

A = Company fails in the right country to select agent or entry mode.
B = Presentation style or content wrong for marketplace.
C = After convincing the buyer of the product's features, benefits,
    and quality, the company fails to convince on secondary issues
D = Even after positive decision is made, company fails to support
    marketplace properly and sales dwindle.
☆ = Critical action required.

┊ = Pitfall areas likely to result in lost business.

Figure 1

PITFALL C – NEGOTIATION

After convincing the buyers of the product's features, benefits, price, and qualify, the company fails to convince on secondary issues.

Secondary issues could be assurances of delivery, quality control, management trust, long term relationship building, etc. Make sure you remember you're selling to emotional needs as well as logical needs. They need to trust you, to like dealing with you, to see long term benefits developing.

PITFALL D – FOLLOW-UP

Even after a positive decision is made, the company fails to support the marketplace properly, and sales dwindle.

Don't expect the market to run without attention any more than you would expect an employee to run without back-up support, and motivation. Make sure to contact the marketplace regularly, perhaps even one time each week from the beginning of the relationship. Use telephone, email, fax, letters, visits, or whatever it takes to get results. Send everything you promise, when you promise. Deliver on time, pay on time, provide training and promotional support.

Remember to succeed in overseas markets:

Wake up to cultural differences.
Do it their way, not yours.

ACTION SHEET
Chapter 24

Ideas for Development:

1. Investigate the style of your foreign competitors and decide if you're in a position to give the market the necessary time and money to cultivate it.
2. When selling overseas remember that building a rapport may be far more important to your sales than it is in your home market.
3. Send the person who can adapt to the overseas business style quickly and has cultural acumen.
4. Beware of the importance of secondary issues such as trust, assurances of prompt delivery, and long term business relationship building.
5. Support the marketplace after selling as seriously as you do the home market.
6. List other points here:
7.
8.

Of the above ideas, which one is likely to yield the best results?

What percentage of sales (or performance) increase could realistically be expected?

How long would it take: to develop the idea? to get results?

Who would have to be involved?

What date should we start?

What is the first step I should take?

PART 8

CONSOLIDATING YOUR FORWARD PLAN

Chapter 25

Responsible -- Who, Me?

In the mid 1700s, Samuel Johnson, the great English writer said, "To do nothing is in everyone's power!"

America's Mark Twain said, "It ain't those parts of the Bible that I can't understand that bother me, it's the parts I do understand."

We often understand what needs to be done in life if we're honest with ourselves, but being the humans that we are, we let obstacles stand in our way. We delay. We make excuses to ourselves. That's human, perhaps. Yet we see that the great achievers reflect on these human failings and take action against them.

DO IT NOW

I remember one evening sitting with my husband watching the story of Gilbert and Sullivan on television. In one scene, Sullivan was in the south of France having a well-deserved rest. The wife of his business manager arrived to extend an invitation from England to him to write two new operas. What did Sullivan do?

Upon hearing the news, he jumped out of his chair in the middle of the hotel lounge, ready to rush off to England. The woman who brought him the news had to urge him to finish his coffee before rushing off, his enthusiasm and eagerness to do it now was so great.

With this attitude, is there any wonder that his works became known around the world?

A client of mine, Julia Davies had a superb sign in her office. It said, "Do it today, for tomorrow it will take twice as long, and next week three times as long." What's worse, as you and I know, is leaving it until another time. This increases the chances of nothing happening. Achievers use enthusiasm, which drives them to immediate action.

Doing it now is harder than it sounds. I was in Cairo shortly after starting my consulting business. I was doing research for Optrex on a pharmaceutical product, and at the end of the project the last thing I wanted to do was to start writing the report. The research was ready, but the task of unraveling it and putting it into words was daunting.

"I won't start now. I'll wait until I get on the plane," I thought. "After all, I deserve a rest and I want to see Cairo, and . . and . . . and . . ." When the 'ands' got up to about 10, I had to start being honest with myself.

"Are you going to take action now?" I asked myself, "or are you going to let the work pile up and make you depressed? You know you won't do it on the plane. And when you get back, your memory of the details will be dull and your inspiration will be even less than it is today."

"Hmm," I said back to myself. "Now that you put it that way, yes, well, I guess I'll do it now."

I still remember that conversation I had with myself, standing in the middle of my hotel room at the Nile Hilton. I did the report. And you can guess what happened, can't you? It went quicker than I expected, and I had time to see Cairo, have the well-deserved rest, and so on.

If I hadn't done the report, I'd have been miserable because it would have hung over my head. And upon my return, I'd be unhappy seeing the new pile of work waiting on my desk, and the report still to do.

Whenever I feel tempted to delay, I think of that day in Cairo. It gives me good memories of the beginning of my pattern to do it now.

PURSUE IMPROVEMENTS EVERYDAY

Ben Franklin dedicated much of his life overcoming what he thought were his personality defects. In his autobiography, printed in 1868, he outlined 13 virtues he pursued each day of the week.

This pursuit didn't stop him from all the other things he did. It didn't stop him from inventing, from politicking, from influencing world events for years to come. He took the time to take responsibility for everything he wanted to achieve in life.

There are pages of proven techniques in this book that, if implemented, will reap tremendous results, results that can transform lives and companies. Yet, nothing will happen if we ourselves don't take responsibility for implementing them.

Over the years, I've worked with almost every imaginable industry. I worked with manufacturers, with service companies, with financiers, with retailers. We've helped them to sell better, to motivate, to plan their future, and to export. We know their companies backwards and forwards.

We could talk about business improvement techniques for weeks and months, but we haven't. We've picked out 25 areas of concentration for you, which we know apply to all businesses and organizations. These 25 areas have been tried and tested in hundreds and hundreds of companies. They've been tried and tested with all levels of people--company presidents and junior personnel--in North and South America, in Europe, in Australia, in Asia.

Even with all this evidence, a few managers from time to time enter our seminars with hesitation. They use a skeptical approach, looking for reasons things won't work. And that's valid to a point. But if you are that type of person by nature, don't let your skepticism stop you from advancing. It's up to each of us to make things happen.

I like what Christopher Morley said about success: "There is only one success, and that is to be able to spend your life in your own way." You can do this only if you plan for it.

What specific things do you want to achieve in life? How do you want to spend it? Ben Franklin knew it wasn't easy to have everything perfect, so he got a start on it by taking one step at a time. He kept at it. He achieved what he wanted.

As you've read throughout this book, you've probably had a lot of ideas about how you could relate the principles described to your own situation to get the success you want. Which one will you start on first?

START SMALL AND BUILD STEADILY

Our advice is to start step by step. *Choose a principle that you can visualize implementing easily. Choose one that will bring results quickly. Then build on it.*

If you choose an achievable principle, you'll get results and you'll continue to build. You can refer back to the principles in the book often to continue your building process.

That doesn't mean your goals should be small. Indeed not. Your dream should be big. The big picture is made up of small component steps. Remember the section on management controls? We said that it was important to analyze results in specific segments. The same is true with carrying out your forward plan. Take it segment by segment.

If we want success, we need to apply undying persistence to the things that matter most to us.

FOSTER RESPONSIBILITY

If we want to achieve our goals, other people will be important. How will we keep them motivated to take responsibility, to overcome the obstacles that stand in the way?

Ian McCallum has a technique that is very effective. Ian, like other successful directors we know, has an appetite for new ideas. He prepares himself by trying new ideas and integrating them in his working style. What better way is there to motivate employees than to set an example!

I met Ian one day at the airport near our office on his flight back from a business meeting. He said he had learned a very good management technique from dealing with my company.

At our first meeting, he said, our project manager Angus Garfield had gone through a list of what we had expected from that meeting. Ian felt that was a very effective way to begin a meeting and had used it at his meeting--leading his customer through a point-by-point agenda. The result was immensely successful and Ian was determined to use it in all future meetings.

SET THE EXAMPLE

Ian believes that people look to their boss for ideas, and how right he is! If the boss is willing to take responsibility for better ways of doing things, it sets an example for all. If we want to instill responsibility in others, shouldn't we show them the way?

Angus Garfield, who gave Ian this idea, was a person who always commanded the respect of clients several years his senior. Angus knew his areas of strength and pursued them. What was his major strength? Enthusiasm.

Whenever people at the office missed their targets or had a bad day, Angus was the first to say, "Cheer up, tomorrow will bring success." He was always the one to congratulate people for doing a job well. "You really handled that well," he'd say. No wonder Ian liked his approach to the point-by-point agenda.

Would he have liked Angus's methods if Angus had presented the idea without the right attitude? Without enthusiasm? Probably not.

Angus commanded leadership. He took responsibility by using his best asset--enthusiasm, What are the best assets of your people? Find them and you'll find the key to fostering responsibility.

REMEMBER THE IMPORTANCE OF TRAINING

Training is another important part of preparing ourselves and others for responsibility. Itsu Yamamoto, in Tokyo, told me that training a person for management is no different than training a part of the body. When we learn to throw a ball, the arm learns to move efficiently in a certain way, just as the legs learn to walk.

And so it is in management. Training, he says, is an ongoing process. Itsu meets with his people on a regular basis. He expects them to learn his philosophy as well as the practices of the company.

In his business of importing products and selling to the Japanese market, there must be a trust built up between himself and his customer. Therefore every detail must be known to employees dealing with an account. Mr. Yamamoto wants his people to take responsibility and so he gives them the skill they need.

What other steps can we take to overcome that obstacle of responsibility? I particularly liked the philosophy that former UCLA Coach John Wooden taught his award-winning basketball teams who won national championships year after year: "I will get ready, and then perhaps my chance will come." Should we take responsibility for our own training or should we wait for others to prepare us? We know what Coach Wooden would say. The fact is that it's up to us to get ready.

REINFORCE EVERYONE'S DISTINCTIVE COMPETENCE

Jim Kearns goes by the 'distinctive competence' doctrine. He gets to know his people well, in order to help them identify their distinctive competence. "Do better what you do best" is one of Jim's mottoes. Despite heavy travel commitments Jim takes time to get to know his people. He helps them recognize their distinctive competence. When they know what they're best at, they take responsibility.

The same was true of the management trainees. As they recorded two successes per day, they gained an understanding of their ability. They reinforced their ability to succeed.

Do whatever it takes for you to succeed. Talk to yourself. Make notes to remind yourself. Listen to your principles on a cassette as you drive to work. Keep on course. Take Morley's advice and set your forward plan and work step by step to achieve your success and to spend your life in your own way.

Remember to consolidate your forward plan:

Set goals and build on them relentlessly. Motivate yourself by focusing on the results and the benefits you'll gain.

Write to us and let us know how you implement the principles.

Wishing you all the best of success,

Christine Harvey
Email: ChristineHarvey@compuserve.com
Website: www.ChristineHarvey.com
Tel US: (520) 325-8733, Fax US: (520) 325-8743
Tel UK: 01895-431 471, Fax UK: 01895-422 565

Bill Sykes
Email: WASykes@aol.com
Tel UK: 01666-824 211
Fax UK: 01666-825 229

ACTION SHEET
Chapter 25

Ideas for Development:

1. Choose a principle you can visualize implementing and start there.
2. Dream big, but segment into small workable pieces.
3. Foster responsibility in others by setting an example.
4. Go by the motto, "I will prepare myself and then my chance will come."
5. Discover the distinctive competence of each person and build on that strength.
6. List other points here:
7.
8.

Of the above ideas, which one is likely to yield the best results?

What percentage of sales (or performance) increase could realistically be expected?

How long would it take: to develop the idea? to get results?

Who would have to be involved?

What date should we start?

What is the first step I should take?

INDEX

Books and tapes by Christine Harvey

Can A Girl Run For President?
Use the world as your arena as you develop your leadership. Step-by-step methods and advice for getting to the top by women around the world. Overcome limitations and reach your full potential. $14.95

Secret's of the World's Top Sales Performers
Ten people in 10 industries in 10 countries give you unique perspectives that can easily be adapted to your needs. A must for sales and non-sales people alike. 150,000 copies in 5 languages. $6.95

In Pursuit of Profit: Christine Harvey
with Bill Sykes
If you are in management, sales, run your own company, or simply want to advance, this book will help you. Pointers from hundreds of industries worldwide. 140,000 copies—8 languages. $14.95

Successful Selling
Looking for a new way to handle objections and closings? Would self-motivation and support systems really keep you going? Proven answers to these and other roadblocks. In 12 languages. $6.95
Successful Motivation
Do you want to motivate yourself and others to new

levels? Seven methods for dealing with situations from difficult people to procrastination to raising productivity and job performance. $14.95

Public Speaking and Leadership Building
Pick this book up and use the methods today. Every situation for the beginner and the pro. Increase your ability step-by-step as your fears dissolve. In 5 languages.
Workbook format. $89.95

Power Talk
Video or Audio
Powerful speaking and leadership techniques.
V – $39.95 / A – $14.95

Can A Girl Run For President?
Video or Audio
Christine Harvey's speech to American GS Leaders of Europe.
V – $39.95 / A – $14.95

3 Steps to Business and Personal Success – **Audio**
Interview with top sales performer Janet Lim, and a motivating speech about the Secrets of the World's Top Sales Performers. $14.95

Quick Order Form

Fax order: 1-520-325-8743 and send this form.

Telephone orders: 1-877-731-6045 with credit card

Website Orders: Visit www.ChristineHarvey.com.

Mail To: Intrinsic Publishing, P.O. Box 26040, Tucson, AZ 85726 USA.

Please send the following books and tapes. I understand that I may return any of them for a full refund – no questions asked.

Books:

Qty: ___ Can A Girl Run for President? $14.95

Qty: ___ Secret's of the World's Top Sales Performers $6.95

Qty: ___ In Pursuit of Profit $14.95

Qty: ___ Successful Selling $6.95

Qty: ___ Successful Motivation $14.95

Qty: ___ Public Speaking and Leadership Workbook $89.95

Tapes: (V = video) or (A = audio)

Qty: ___ Power Talk: V – $39.95 / A – $14.95

Qty: ___ Can A Girl Run For President?: V – $39.95 / A – $14.95

Qty: ___ 3 Steps to Business and Personal Success: A – $14.95

⍟⍟⍟⍟⍟⍟

NAME: _____

ADDRESS: _____

CITY: _____ **STATE:** _____

ZIP/POST CODE: _____ **COUNTRY:** _____

E-MAIL ADDRESS: _____

TELEPHONE: _____ **OR FAX** _____

In case of shipping or order questions, we may need to contact you. Please list either email, telephone or fax; email preferred.

SALES TAX: Add 7% for books shipped to an Arizona address.

DISCOUNTS: *10% for 2 or more of the same title in books or tapes.*

SHIPPING BY AIR FOR US: $4 for first book/tape; $2 for each add'l.

FOR INTERNATIONAL: $9 for first book/tape; $5 for each add'l.

PAYMENT: ❑ Check or ❑ Card __VISA __M/C __AMEX

Card number: _____

Name on Card: _____ Exp. Date: ___ / ___

Would You Like To Have Christine Harvey Speak to Your Group?

Simply fill in this form.
Fax to: (520) 325-8743
E-Mail to: ChristineHarvey@
CompuServe.com
Or Call: (520) 325-8733
Website:
www.ChristineHarvey.com

Subject Possibilities...

Secrets of the World's Top Sales Performers
...From her book about 10 top sales achievers in 10 industries in 10 countries

Three Ways to Raise Your Credibility
...Learn the secrets of gaining leadership positions, raising your profile and influence

Power Talk
...From her 40- part TV communication and leadership series

Can a Girl Run for President?
...Raising your own leadership and credibility while helping society

Name _____
_____

Tel_____

Fax _____

Email _____
_____

Group _____